PREJUDENTIAL

Black America and the Presidents

MARGARET KIMBERLEY

T2P

TRUTH TO POWER

an imprint of

STEERFORTH PRESS
LEBANON, NEW HAMPSHIRE

For information about permission to reproduce
selections from this book, write to:
Steerforth Press L.L.C., 31 Hanover Street, Suite 1
Lebanon, New Hampshire 03766

Cataloging-in-Publication Data is available from the Library of Congress

Printed in the United States of America

ISBN 978-1-58642-248-6

1 3 5 7 9 10 8 6 4 2

To my parents

VERA NARED WALTON and CALVIN WALTON

CONTENTS

PREFACE

In 1956, I shall not go to the polls. I have not registered. I believe that democracy has so far disappeared in the United States that no "two evils" exist.
There is but one evil party with two names, and it
will be elected despite all I can do or say.[1]

— W. E. B. Du Bois, 1956

Once upon a time there were millions of people living on a continent. They were invaded by people from a distant part of the world.
These newcomers killed the inhabitants via military attacks, infec-
tious diseases, and outright theft of their lands. The invaders also
kidnapped other human beings from yet another part of the world
and enslaved them on the stolen land. More than two hundred
years after the invaders appeared there was a war that ended slavery but accelerated the extermination of the indigenous residents.
More invaders came until they had claimed the entire continent.
The political and economic system of this land was built on these
crimes.

These are undeniable truths of American history that can be
asserted and summed up briefly, but the devil is always in the
details. Americans like to think of themselves as an exceptional
people bound together by noble ideals. This belief is challenged,
however, when history is taught more honestly and fully, without
omitting facts or telling outright lies. Presidents are outsized char-
acters in America's narrative about itself. Children attend schools
named after them; there are monuments dedicated to them in
every state. They have their own national holiday, Presidents'
Day, which presents an opportunity for the country's virtues to

be celebrated. We are conditioned to feel a deep connection to these men hundreds of years after some of them have died.

The language used to create and protect presidential images is telling. The first several presidents are known as the Founding Fathers, a term that affirms patriarchy and white supremacy. George Washington is more than just the first president; he is the "Father of Our Country." Regardless of our group affiliations and histories, we are taught to see these people as benevolent figures, no matter what actions they took while in office.

Most Americans are taught from childhood, for instance, that George Washington and Thomas Jefferson were brave and brilliant men in any number of ways, but the fact that both men owned human beings as slaves is rarely mentioned in telling their stories or assessing their character. Americans are not taught that the British offered freedom to the enslaved people who fought on their side in the Revolutionary War. Abraham Lincoln, widely regarded as the great liberator, initially sought to limit the spread of slavery, rather than to end it, and actively considered the option of deporting or segregating black people to make America a whites-only society. Franklin Roosevelt and John Kennedy are considered to have been "good for black people," even though they constantly feared antagonizing southern segregationists and failed their constituents.

It is particularly difficult to write about America's history without giving in to the notion of patriotism, which includes suppressing certain narratives. Even those who think of themselves as progressives base their arguments for systemic change in terms of obedience to the cherished myths of great men. Despite claims to the contrary, Americans are highly indoctrinated in the belief of American superiority. Though the democratic progress usually amounts to a series of compromises and incremental steps, emphasizing only those facts of history that make our "great men" look good undermines the creation of the sense of inclusion and understanding necessary to improve the lives of all citizens.

This book is an effort to shed light on the truth. George Washington didn't have wooden teeth, as is commonly believed, but he did take teeth out of his slaves' mouths. He may not have chopped down a cherry tree, but when Philadelphia became the capital of the United States, he deliberately rotated his slaves out of Pennsylvania so as to avoid their becoming emancipated, as the law would have required.

The very foundation of this country, the celebrated Declaration of Independence from Great Britain, was tainted by the fact that some delegates to the Second Continental Congress were keenly focused on the continuation of slavery. The case in which James Somerset, who was brought to London by his Bostonian slave-holder, was freed in 1772 threatened the future of slaveholding in the thirteen colonies. He won his freedom based on the argument that the law of England did not support slavery. Many feared that the precedent might "cheat an honest American of his slave."[2]

All of the men who became president were able to reach that high office in part because they swore allegiance to American ideals that were built on tenets of conquest and enslavement. These truths are self-evident: The founding of the United States continued the conquest and genocide of the continent's indigenous population and protected the practice of slavery. The legacies of predatory capitalism and anti-black racism are a huge part of our collective story. None of this is ancient history that can be dismissed in the twenty-first century. These themes run deeply in our culture, and they should be acknowledged and understood. Aristotle said: "If liberty and equality, as thought by some, are chiefly to be found in democracy, they will be attained when all persons alike share in government to the utmost." More than twenty-three hundred years later, we're still not there. Americans need to recognize the malignancies that have threatened the healthier aspects of our shared history and continue to do so. If we are ever to have the opportunity to be fully realized as human beings, capable of living in peace among ourselves and the rest of the world, then we need to be honest with ourselves. To the extent that our leaders embody aspects of who we are as a people, studying how each president has participated in our nation's complicated and often shameful treatment of black people is as good a place as any to start.

1789–1825

THE "FOUNDING FATHERS"

1790: Maryland, Massachusetts, New York, North Carolina, Pennsylvania, and Vermont allow free African Americans to vote.

1793: The invention of the cotton gin increases the profitability of slave labor.

1793: A federal fugitive slave law provides for the return of the enslaved who escape and cross state lines.

1800: The US Census shows 893,602 enslaved people in the country.

1808: Congress prohibits the slave trade, but illegal smuggling continues until 1860.

1816: The American Colonization Society is formed to relocate free African Americans to Africa.

1820: The Missouri Compromise bans slavery above 36°30' in latitude.

GEORGE WASHINGTON

1789–1797

Children learn in school that George Washington's false teeth were made of wood. That is not true. Some of his dentures were made of ivory and metal, but some of them came from the human beings he owned. Washington became a slave owner at the age of eleven upon his father's death. He increased his wealth in 1759 when he married Martha Custis, a widow who had nearly three hundred slaves, of which more than eighty were dower slaves — meaning they were granted to her upon her husband's death — while the remainder were in her custody until their minor son came of age to own them legally, while Washington had approximately fifty.

When Washington's dentures became ill fitting and painful, he chose to get teeth from the people he owned. Records show that they were paid 122 shillings for nine teeth — less than a third the going rate at the time. Washington told a friend, "I confess I have been staggered in my belief in the efficacy of transplantion [*sic*]."[1] The payment didn't diminish the terror for the chattel. The fact that Washington owned other people at all was a crime and a grievous one at that. But the "Father of Our Country" didn't see things that way because he did not see black people as fully human, endowed with unalienable rights, and so he did everything in his power to maintain his hold on his living, breathing capital. His story, sanitized for elementary schoolchildren, is a fundamental example of the lies told about our nation's history that keep Americans ignorant of the truth and how it affects them today.

The first capital of the United States was New York City, where Washington was sworn into office in 1789. The Residence Act passed in 1790 mandated that the capital be temporarily moved to Philadelphia for a period of ten years before being permanently established along the Potomac River by 1800.

From the start northern politicians were held hostage by the southern plantation economy. Southerners insisted that the capital be located in a place that was decidedly dependent on the planter economy. The creation of a new capital city was an enormous victory for the slaveholding class. Their peculiar institution was granted physical protection and the imprimatur of a government built to ensure its survival. A central political principle in the early days of this country was the maintenance and protection of the slavery system. However, anyone who believes in American superiority is expected to omit or at least downplay this fact to maintain the illusion of democracy and beneficence.

Even the ten years of governance in Philadelphia proved to be problematic. A 1780 Pennsylvania law guaranteed enslaved people the right to seek their freedom if they remained in the state for more than six months. This could have put Washington in a bind, but he had a solution: He rotated his human property for six-month intervals between Pennsylvania and Virginia. He did this in flagrant violation of a 1788 amendment to this law, which prohibited such actions. In 1791, Washington started by rotating nine people, including a dower slave named Ona Maria "Oney"

Judge. In a letter to his secretary, Tobias Lear, Washington mused on the slaves' potential access to freedom.

> At any rate it might, if they conceived they had a right to it, make them insolent in a State of Slavery. As all except Hercules and Paris are dower negroes, it behooves me to prevent the emancipation of them, otherwise I *shall* not only loose [*sic*] the use of them, but may have them to pay for. If upon taking good advice it is found expedient to send them back to Virginia, I wish to have it accomplished under pretext that may deceive both them and the Public.[2]

Washington was serious about denying any opportunity for freedom. Oney Judge recalled her escape in an 1845 interview: "Whilst they were packing up to go to Virginia, I was packing to go, I didn't know where; for I knew that if I went back to Virginia, I should never get my liberty. I had friends among the colored people of Philadelphia, had my things carried there beforehand, and left Washington's house while they were eating dinner."[3] Oney managed to flee to New Hampshire in 1796, but she still was not safe. The Fugitive Slave Clause in the Constitution allowed for her to be returned to bondage, and the Washingtons tried incessantly to get her back. With more than three hundred human beings among their collective property, the escape of even one might put the entire enterprise on shaky ground.

A friend of the Washingtons saw Judge in New Hampshire and informed them. The president wrote a letter to his secretary of the Treasury, Oliver Wolcott, demanding his assistance in getting Judge back. "I am sorry to give you, or anyone else, trouble on such a trifling occasion, but the ingratitude of the girl, who was brought up and treated more like a child than a Servant (and Mrs. Washington's desire to recover her) ought not to escape with impunity if it can be avoided."[4]

Washington sent intermediaries to try to trick Judge into return-
ing with promises of freedom. Those promises were lies; as a dower
slave she could not have been freed without compensation given
to the Custis estate, and the Washingtons' determination to recapture her is an indication that they were unlikely to even contem-
plate such an effort. She avoided the attempts to entrap her and
remained a free woman for the rest of her life.

Not only did Washington not allow any of his slaves to go free,
but he also did not countenance other white people doing things
that might lessen his hold on this property. Sally Green was the
abandoned wife of an overseer on Washington's Mount Vernon
estate. When Washington learned in 1794 that she planned to open
a small store in Alexandria he was not pleased, and he wrote to
his manager, William Pearce: "Caution Sally Green against dealing
with my negroes after she is fixed in Alexandria. If she deals with
them at all she will be unable to distinguish between stolen, or not
stolen things; and if her conduct should lay her open to suspicion
she need expect no further countenance or support from me."[5]

A great irony exists in the fact that *Washington* is now the
"blackest" surname in the United States. Ninety percent of the
Washingtons in America are black people. It is not clear how
many of them may be descended from Washington or the enslaved
people on his estate. Booker T. Washington claimed to have chosen
the name randomly when he was a child.[6] Most of the ancestors of
today's Washingtons probably chose the name as a way of identify-
ing themselves with their country, a major irony in the face of what
black people have had to contend with throughout this country's
history.

George Washington would express some reservations about
slavery, exclaiming at one point that he wanted "to be quit of
negroes," yet he never freed any in his lifetime. He did not have
the right to free Martha's dower slaves or those who belonged to
the estate of her first husband, Daniel Parke Custis. But in his will

he did agree to free those he owned after Martha's death. This left his widow, Martha, afraid that she could be killed by people who would gain their freedom if she died. Abigail Adams said as much after a visit with her in 1800: "In the state in which they were left by the General, to be free at her death, she did not feel as tho her Life was safe in their Hands, many of whom would be told that it was there [sic] interest to get rid of her — She therefore was advised to set them all free at the close of the year."⁷ Martha decided to manumit, or free, the slaves belonging to her late second husband, George Washington. But her dower slaves — those she received from her first husband's estate — never gained their freedom. Upon her death they were dispersed among her grandchildren, splitting up numerous families in the process.

Washington was followed in the office of president by eleven other slaveholding men, seven of whom owned slaves even while holding that office. Their slave ownership was not incidental to their achieving the highest office in the land but was inextricably linked to that fact. Slaveholding was profitable, and it is logical that the elite classes of that time would be represented in presidential contests. The United States was committed to maintaining this institution, and whether northern or southern, no president considered ending the practice until Abraham Lincoln was forced to confront the matter in 1861.

JOHN ADAMS

1797–1801

Of the first twelve presidents, John Adams and his son John Quincy Adams were the only two who were northerners and non-slaveholding, but the elder Adams was far more pro-white than he was anti-slavery. He expressed racist views early in his life and took part in the shameful libel of a dead black man to win a court case. Adams represented the British soldiers who took part in the 1770 Boston Massacre. Crispus Attucks, a man who had escaped slavery, was the first victim to fall on that day. Adams's defense strategy included blaming Attucks, ". . . to whose mad behavior, in all probability, the dreadful carnage of that night is chiefly to be ascribed."[1] Adams also represented slaveholders in four cases in which enslaved people sued for their freedom. He lost three of the four and later wrote dismissively, "I was concerned in several Causes in which Negroes sued for their Freedom before the Revolution."[2] He felt more angst on behalf of white southerners than he did for enslaved people, and he asserted that "the condition of the common sort of white people" was "more oppressed, degraded, and miserable than that of the negroes."[3]

Adams bragged that he had never held a slave, though he could have done so in Massachusetts for most of his life. Despite his self-congratulation on the subject, he didn't think slavery was so terrible that it needed to end, and he made clear that he avoided "animated speeches [and] inflammatory publications"[4] expressing opposition to the institution. He was concerned about the prospect of black people, whether free or enslaved, rising up violently against whites. Adams feared black freedom more than he thought that slavery was wrong, and he argued that "the abolition of slavery must be gradual, and accomplished with much caution and circumspection. Violent measures would produce greater violations of justice and humanity than the continuance of the practice . . . would probably excite insurrections among the blacks to rise against their masters, and imbue their hands in innocent blood."[5]

Adams identified with his fellow white people, particularly white southerners, with whom he promised not to interfere. "The present slaveholders cannot justly be reproached. They have given proofs of dispositions favorable to the gradual abolition of slavery, more explicit than could have been expected."[6]

Like many presidents who followed him, Adams favored colonization, the forced removal of black people from the United States. Thirty years after the end of the Revolutionary War, he condemned the British for again giving freedom to enslaved people who fought for them, this time in the War of 1812.

> Instead of leaving the stolen Negroes to Starve in Halifax and London or Sending them to Sierra Leona, they have now planted a Colony of them in Nova Scotia. A thousand Families are established in one Settlement, with ten Acres of Land granted by the Crown to each

with an Allowance of Instruments and Provisions for two Years. From this Nursery are hereafter to be drawn recruits to invade the Southern States to entice and Seduce other blacks to desert or rebel against their Masters and the Nation.[7]

John Adams has been damned with faint praise for never owning slaves, but his fear of black people and their continued presence in the country explains why he and his northern brethren bent over backward to adhere to the demands of the slavocracy. Adams wanted black people to be kept subservient or, better yet, kept out of the country altogether. Adams and other northerners weren't that different from their slaveholding countrymen in their feelings of racial superiority. They saw black people as irritants and inconveniences at best, and murderers at worst. They had no inclination at all to advocate for the enslaved — Adams admitted as much.

Adams did not change in the years after his term in office ended. He continued to fear the presence of black people, and he saw no value in giving them their freedom. In an 1814 letter he predicted that emancipation would end with "the shiftless perishing from want" or "asking their old aristocratical masters [to take them back]" or "inroads, depredations and brigandages."[8]

Even after declaring himself "utterly averse to admission of slavery into the Missouri territory"[9] in an 1821 letter, he didn't want to say so publicly. He feared that his son John Quincy's political career might be damaged by "heated prejudiced minds of southern people." He begged his friend, "I hope you will by no means publish my letter."[10]

Perhaps Adams felt the fact that he never owned another human being absolved him from needing to express any pro-emancipation opinion. He could be honest in his antipathy toward black people — unlike his successors Thomas Jefferson and James Madison, who engaged in breathtaking hypocrisies.

THOMAS JEFFERSON

1801–1809

Jefferson presents a contradiction for the apologists and idol worshippers. For obvious reasons they admire his erudition and scholarship, but they cannot sugarcoat the fact that he owned more than six hundred human beings during his life and had sex with at least one of them when she was a minor child. Yet he also claimed to have misgivings about slavery. Thomas Jefferson was the worst kind of hypocrite on this topic — and one who defined his time, because his wealth depended on his ownership of human beings. Jefferson said that he wanted the gradual abolition of slavery, but during his lifetime he freed only two of the people he owned, and only five more in his will. It should no longer be acceptable to overlook the profit Jefferson made from involvement in a cruel and barbaric industry.

The early presidents established the mandate to expand feverishly westward, relentlessly occupying Indian land and turning it over to the white settler population. Jefferson is credited — if such a positive word can be used — with transacting the Louisiana Purchase.

The United States doubled in size in 1803 when France agreed to sell off the last of its territories on the North American mainland. The 827,000 square miles of territory west of the Mississippi comprised what are now Arkansas, Missouri, Iowa, Oklahoma, Kansas, Nebraska, and portions of Minnesota, North Dakota, South Dakota, New Mexico, Texas, Montana, Wyoming, Colorado, and, of course, Louisiana. The sale was driven by the French need for money after the loss of their extremely profitable plantation economy in the wake of a successful Haitian slave revolt. The ultimate irony is that the end of Haitian slavery increased the amount of territory that would be available to the American plantation economy. The purchase included lands still inhabited by indigenous people, most of whom had no idea that France had claimed ownership of their homes or that the United States now "possessed" them.

Jefferson, who ostensibly held the opinion that slavery was evil and unjust, could have forbidden the practice in the newly acquired territories when in March 1804, Congress gave him full executive, judicial, and legislative power over them. He drafted the territorial constitution himself. The original treaty giving the United States jurisdiction asserted that "inhabitants of the ceded territory" would enjoy the same rights as all American citizens; Jefferson changed the wording to "white inhabitants."[1]

Jefferson saw this expanse of land in part as a gigantic Indian reservation to which he could forcibly relocate the remaining members of the eastern Native American tribes. He told William Henry Harrison, a future president and the governor of the Indiana Territory at that time: "Should any tribe be foolhardy enough to take up the hatchet at any time, the seizing [of] the whole country of that tribe, and driving them across the Mississippi, as the only condition of peace, would be an example to others, and a furtherance of our final consolidation."[2]

Had Jefferson wanted to end the evil of slavery he could have done it with the stroke of a pen. He could have gone the route of the reformist "post-natal" emancipation plans whereby persons born on or after a certain date were freed at a certain age. (His 1783 draft of a constitution for the state of Virginia contained a provision that would have emancipated those born after December 31, 1800. The draft language was absent from the final document.) Jefferson did nothing of the sort, and in fact he supported the continuing expansion of slavery. He saw slavery as beneficial to white people, but he tried to hide this belief by advocating the dubious "dispersion" theory, which held that if slavery were dispersed throughout the country it would end more quickly on a state-by-state basis. A visitor to Monticello in 1820 wrote of Jefferson's determination to make the new Louisiana territories safe for slavery.

> Among other political points, that which has been called the Missouri question stood prominent. He said that nothing had happened since the revolution, which gave him so much anxiety and so many disquieting fears for the safety and happiness of his country. "I fear," said he, "that much mischief has been done already, but if they carry matters to extremities again at the approaching session of Congress, nothing short of Almighty power can save us. The Union will be broken. All the horrors of Civil War, embittered by local jealousies and mutual recriminations, will ensue. Bloodshed, rapine and cruelty will soon roam at large, will desolate our once happy land and turn the fruitful field into a howling wilderness. Out of such a state of things will naturally grow a war of extermination toward the African in our land. Instead of improving the condition of this poor, afflicted, degraded race, terminating, in the ordering of wisdom, in equal liberty and the enjoyment of equal rights (in which direction public opinion is advancing with rapid strides) the course pursued, by those who

make high professions of humanity and of friendship for them, would involve them as well as us in certain destruction."[3]

The Missouri question, which led to the 1820 Missouri Compromise establishing which states would allow or prohibit slavery, would ultimately push the nation to war, and Jefferson foresaw as much. The Union would be "broken" if anti-slavery forces didn't quiet themselves and disappear. Jefferson predicted civil war, but he could not comprehend the defeat of the slavocracy, only the destruction of black people.

Before the Louisiana Purchase was finalized, Jefferson, James Madison, and George Washington made sure that the nation's capital remained in slave territory. It is true that Alexander Hamilton made a deal to assume the war debts of the new states in exchange for moving the capital from New York farther south to Philadelphia and then to a newly created city wedged between Maryland and Virginia. But that transaction was hardly the primary motivation. A federal capital carved out of territory taken from existing states could have been located elsewhere. The rationale for creating an entirely new city, located on a swamp no less, in slave territory was to give slavery legal and physical protection. The choice made little sense unless one acknowledges the importance of slavery to the growth and development of the American economy.

Jefferson certainly knew its importance to the settler colonial state and to himself personally. In 1798 his friend Tadeusz Kosciuszko drew up a will asking Jefferson to use his estate to free enslaved people: "I beg Mr. Jefferson that in the case I should die without will or testament he should bye out of my money So many Negroes and free them, that the restante [remaining] sums should be Sufficient to give them aducation and provide for ther maintenance."[4]

He revised the will eighteen years later and made his desires clearer. "I do hereby declare and direct that should I make no other testamentary disposition of my property in the United States I hereby authorize my friend Thomas Jefferson to employ the whole thereof in purchasing Negroes from among his own or any others."[5]

But Jefferson never used the bequest to do anything that Kosciuszko asked. When he died, enslaved persons were sold to pay off his debts. Despite his pretend angst, he was a slaveholder to the very end.

JAMES MADISON

1809–1817

James Madison's last will and testament states in part: "I give and bequeath my ownership in the negroes and people of colour held by me to my dear wife, but it is my desire that none of them should be sold without his or her consent or in case of their misbehaviour; except that infant children may be sold with their parent who consents for them to be sold with him or her, and who consents to be sold."[1] These words sum up the infuriating degree of Madison's hypocrisy. He often called slavery an "evil" and yet he participated in this evil throughout his life. For many years he claimed that he would free the humans he owned after he died, but his final wishes prove that he had no intention of doing so. His wife, Dolley, was the daughter of a Quaker who had freed enslaved people in 1783, but after her husband died she sold hers to pay off debts. She did not follow the request in her husband's will that she ask their permission to sell them, as her cousin Edward Coles shared in a letter to his sister: "The poor creatures wd: run to the house and protest agst. Being sold, & say their old master had said in his will that they were not to be sold but with their consent. She sold while I was with her a woman and 2 children to her Nephew Ambrose Madison who lives near her. The woman protested agst. being sold & the more so as her husband was not sold with her."[2]

Like Thomas Jefferson, the slaveholding Madison claimed to think that the institution was wrong, but he never stopped profiting from it personally, and he made sure that his heirs did likewise. His contradiction in thinking slavery evil yet participating in it was resolved by his advocacy for colonization, the removal of black people from the land claimed by whites.

In 1789, Madison wrote "Memorandum on an African Colony for Freed Slaves." He called enslaved people "unhappy" yet assumed that black people would exhibit "vices" whether enslaved or free. Madison also gave credence to the justification of white prejudices against black people and concluded that the "Coast of Africa'" was the best place for what he called a "benevolent experiment."[3] Thirty years later Madison further developed his thinking on the subject and calculated the cost of compensating slaveholders at an estimated six hundred million dollars.[4]

All of Madison's calculations regarding colonization were a sham. Madison and the rest of the slaveholding class were not content to continue owning humans merely for their own comfort and profit; they wanted to expand this business as far as they could. Madison continued the work of his predecessor by grabbing more territory, claiming West Florida as an American territory in 1810 by arguing that it was meant to have been included as part of the Louisiana Purchase. And even those close to Madison apparently did not trust his pro-manumission rhetoric. Consider the case of Edward Coles.

Coles was Dolley Madison's cousin and served as private secretary to Presidents Jefferson and Madison. Like the two presidents he was a Virginia slaveholder, but unlike them he had seriously considered giving his enslaved people their freedom. When Coles inherited twelve people after his father's death he kept silent lest his plans be thwarted. Ten years later, when he informed his family of his plans, they convinced him not to tell his slaves for fear that they would talk and inform other slaves. It took another ten years for Coles to take decisive action, moving with them to Illinois where he assisted them in settling on land he had purchased.

Coles did not tell the six adults and eleven children that they were to be freed until they had left Virginia. Near Pittsburgh, Pennsylvania, en route to Illinois, he told them they were free. "They stared at me and at each other, as if doubting the accuracy or reality of what they heard."[5]

Madison was a hand-wringing hypocrite on the subject of enslavement and any possibility of large-scale manumission. He became chairman of the American Colonization Society in 1833 at the age of eighty-two. He spent the last years of his life claiming that he wanted to stop doing what he had done all his life, but his words were hollow, and he and his family continued their participation in the awful and peculiar institution.

JAMES MONROE

1817–1825

James Monroe was the last of the Founding Fathers to be elected president. Like Washington, Jefferson, and Madison, he was a Virginian and a slaveholder, owning seventy-five persons.[1] Monroe presided over further expansion of the country with the purchase of the remaining Florida Territory from Spain and began the removal of American Indians in the Southeast. He played a role in many horrible events that resonate today.

In 1817, President Monroe and his partner in crime, General Andrew Jackson, decided to kill two birds with one stone. They plotted to attack Seminole Indians in Florida Territory who were aiding escaped slaves from Georgia, Alabama, and South Carolina. In doing so they also established American designs on this Spanish territory.[2] Jackson invaded Florida, captured a Spanish fort at St. Marks, deposed the Spanish governor in Pensacola, and executed two British citizens accused of aiding the Spanish.[3] The incursion created a stir in Washington, but Jackson was never punished. Secretary of State John Quincy Adams defended Jackson. The attack gave Adams the leverage he needed to force Spain to cede that territory to the United States.

Monroe denied giving Jackson permission to invade Florida, but more significant now is the role that historians play in covering up this and other crimes committed by US presidents. Jackson made the case in a letter to Monroe that the invasion could be carried out "without implicating the government." Instead of pointing out that Jackson was acting in accord with the interests and goals of the government, historians advance Monroe's implausible claim that he never saw the letter because "Monroe didn't have a secretary at the time and was ill and didn't read the letter until a year later when Congress was investigating Jackson's actions."[4]

Like most white Americans of his day, Monroe was fearful of the presence of the minority black population who were free. He and other slaveholders, including Andrew Jackson and Francis Scott Key, established the Society for the Colonization of Free People of Color of America in 1816 with the goal of sending the free black population out of the country. It eventually became known as the American Colonization Society (ACS).

A historical irony exists in the fact that Monroe's role in the founding of the ACS led to his name being forever linked to that of an African country. Liberia's capital, Monrovia, is named for a man who kept black people enslaved and wanted others to be shipped off so they wouldn't interfere with the justifications for human ownership.

At the same time that Monroe was promoting settler colonialism, he also oversaw the expansion of slavery in the recently acquired territories. The Missouri Compromise of 1820 did two things: It admitted two states into the Union — Maine as a state that prohibited slavery and Missouri as one allowing it — and it limited slavery to those portions of the Louisiana Purchase below 36°30' latitude, with the exception of Missouri. These machina-

tions kept in place the precarious balance that allowed northerners to think of themselves as enlightened and gave southerners the
incentive to ask for more.

Monroe was infamous for many reasons. He was a slaveholder,
accelerated the theft of indigenous lands to hasten the spread of
slavery, and declared that all of the Western Hemisphere — North,
Central, and South America — was the domain of the United
States. The policy that came to be known as the Monroe Doctrine
was buried in the annual message to Congress on December 2,
1823: "The occasion has been judged proper for asserting, as a
principle in which the rights and interests of the United States are
involved, that the American continents, by the free and independent condition which they have assumed and maintain, are hence-
forth not to be considered as subjects for future colonization by
any European powers."[5]

In other words, any further efforts by Europe to colonize parts
of the Americas would be treated as acts of aggression. The
immediate target of the Monroe Doctrine was the Holy Alliance
of monarchies in the post-Napoleonic era of Europe. Historians
have characterized the policy as the world's only liberal democracy, the United States, taking a stand against autocracy. But it
must be remembered that at this time free blacks did not enjoy
equal protections and rights, and the millions of enslaved were
regarded as property with no rights at all. Moreover, future
American presidents would repeatedly cite the doctrine to
support and justify US aggression. The Eisenhower administration used it to justify a coup against the democratically elected
government of Jacobo Arbenz in Guatemala in 1954. Ronald
Reagan used it in an effort to subvert left-wing governments in
Central America.

In 2019, Donald Trump's national security adviser John Bolton
asserted in an interview that the US would have the right to
take action against leftist governments in Venezuela, Cuba, and

Nicaragua simply because they are in the Western Hemisphere. "In this administration," he said, "we're not afraid to use the word 'Monroe Doctrine.'"[6] A legacy that ought to have been thoroughly discredited is instead used to commit aggressions nearly two hundred years later.

1826–1861

PRE–CIVIL WAR

1830: The Indian Removal Act forces southeastern tribes to leave their native lands, opening them to white settlement and expansion of the plantation economy.

1831: William Lloyd Garrison begins publishing *The Liberator*, a weekly newspaper that advocates the complete abolition of slavery.

1831: Nat Turner, an enslaved African American preacher, leads the most significant slave uprising in American history.

1839: Fifty-three Africans on board the slave ship *Amistad* revolt against their captors, killing all but two crew members.

1851: Sojourner Truth gives her famous "Ain't I a Woman" speech at a convention for women's rights.

1857: The *Dred Scott* decision denies citizenship to all black people.

1859: John Brown's raid on Harpers Ferry, Virginia, sets the stage for the Civil War.

1860: Maine, New Hampshire, Vermont, Rhode Island, and Massachusetts allow free black people to vote.

1860: There are about 4.4 million black people in the United States, and 448,000 are considered "freemen."

JOHN QUINCY ADAMS

1825–1829

President John Quincy Adams, like his father, was nominally opposed to slavery but often took actions that instead expanded its reach. When in the Senate, for instance, he supported the Louisiana Purchase, which increased the size of the slaveholding regions. As secretary of state under President James Monroe, he supported Andrew Jackson's invasion of Florida, even as other cabinet members condemned it. He was also the architect of the Monroe Doctrine. However, he did oppose the annexation of Texas and the subsequent war against Mexico expressly because he knew that these actions were meant to expand slavery.

Following his presidency, Adams distinguished himself in the rhetorical fight against slavery as a member of the House of Representatives from 1831 to 1848. As there weren't many true abolitionists, the most that could be expected of Adams or most white people during this time was that they opposed the spread of slavery. He made a name for himself as a staunch opponent of the gag rule, which at this time prevented discussion or debate in Congress on the issue of slavery by automatically tabling any such petition brought before them without discussion or referral to committee. A Virginia political rival called him "the acutest, the astutest, the archest enemy of southern slavery that ever existed."[1] That description comes with a caveat that any inconvenience to the slavocracy was treated as abolition. Adams and others wanted to make slave trading illegal in Washington, DC, and brought other motions to the House. Adams used anti-slavery petitions in his defense, thereby allowing himself to be censured for violating the gag rule. Under his leadership the rule finally came to an end in 1844.

Adams held a northerner's point of view during his time in political office: He was an accommodationist on the issue of slavery. For too long people like Adams have been given credit that they didn't deserve. While abolitionists began to speak openly about ending slavery, people like Adams considered themselves revolutionary by talking about incremental changes that limited the practice of slaveholding, even though they did not do anything substantive to end the practice.

Adams made numerous statements about the evil of slavery, but he always added that it couldn't end unless the people who profited from it would agree to end it, writing in an 1839 letter to *The National Intelligencer*:

> I desire not to interfere with the institutions of slavery where they are established — I would not abolish slavery without a due regard to indemnify the slaveholder for his loss, and, to avoid the necessity for that, would begin the process with a generation yet unborn. I adhere to the stipulations of the Constitution of the United States, which I have pledged my faith to support; and I can lend my hand to no project for the abolition of slavery in these United States without the consent of their masters.[2]

Despite being callow, his prediction was correct: The slaveholders would not give up their chattel without a bloody fight. Adams and his ilk merely put off the day of reckoning.

Adams himself moved from saying that slaveholders were kind to saying that slavery was a great evil that would end, but only by first breaking the nation apart. He thought it unlikely that the Missouri Compromise would end debate over slavery, writing in 1820: "The President thinks this question will be winked away by a compromise. But so do not I. Much am I mistaken if it is not destined to survive his political and individual life and mine."[3] Instead he called the Missouri Compromise "a mere preamble — a title page to a great tragic volume."

Adams's most positive role in US history took place years after his defeat by Andrew Jackson in the 1828 election. In 1839 the Spanish schooner *Amistad* held newly captured Africans in Cuba. As it prepared to sail from one part of that island to another, the captives, led by a man named Cinque, took control of the ship, killed all but two crew members, and directed the survivors to return them to their homeland. The sailors did not navigate toward Africa and instead went north to the United States, where the ship was captured off the coast of Connecticut. Adams argued for the Africans in the 1841 Supreme Court case that gave Cinque and the others their freedom. He certainly deserves some credit for that act, but that contribution does not take the place of the timidity and acquiescence of Adams and his fellow northerners in their inaction elsewhere.

While in Congress, Adams led the charge against the annexation of Texas, an issue that was the direct result of slavery expansion. Slaveholding southerners had been migrating to this Mexican province for years in the hope that it would eventually be annexed by the United States. When Mexico abolished slavery in 1829 the migrant slaveholders revolted, and after winning military victory in 1836 they declared themselves to be an independent nation. The

Republic of Texas rewrote its constitution, declared slavery legal, and petitioned to be annexed by the United States. Adams and others managed to delay the inevitable until 1845.

John Quincy Adams was, as apologists say, "a man of his times." He contributed to slavery and conquests by white settlers. On only two occasions — with respect to the *Amistad* case and the annexation of Texas — did he do the right thing, and only after he was no longer president. The truth is that Adams realized, as did his fellow early presidents, that "slavery in a moral sense is an evil; but as connected with commerce it has important uses,"[4] which dictated that their opposition to it would be minimal.

ANDREW JACKSON

1829–1837

Andrew Jackson is one president whose actions repeatedly exemplified all the terrible evils of American history. The slaveholding *génocidaire* was no hypocrite on the subject of slavery: He never claimed that it was an evil institution, and he never supported emancipation of any kind. He actively bought and sold human beings before and after his term as president. It is true that he joined the American Colonization Society, but he was not the only slaveholder to do so, as the purpose of the ACS was to remove the free people of color from America and, in so doing, remove a threat to the slave system.

Jackson is responsible for the removal of indigenous people from the southern states. The invention of the cotton gin in 1794 made slavery enormously profitable in the first half of the nineteenth century. The Indian lands in the South were most suitable for cotton, and its cultivation ensured decades of terror for the enslaved population. White settlers from Virginia, North Carolina, South Carolina, and Georgia demanded the expulsion of the indigenous inhabitants of that land, as their continued presence was an obstacle to settlement and the establishment of a plantation economy. The Treaty of Fort Jackson in 1814 forced the indigenous Muscogee tribe to cede twenty-three million acres of land in what was then known as West Florida, which became the territory and state of Alabama. The people's fate was sealed when President Jackson signed the Indian Removal Act in 1830 and they were forcibly exiled, along the infamous Trail of Tears, from their homelands to reservations designated Indian Territory west of the Mississippi River in what is now Oklahoma.

Removal was the beginning of a long history of extreme suffering for the indigenous people in the Southeast, who died from disease and from violence when they attempted to resist subjugation. The domestic slave trade then sent thousands of people from the uppermost slave states to the cotton plantations of the Deep South. The population of Alabama swelled from just ten thousand in 1810 to more than nine hundred thousand in 1860, with half of that population comprising enslaved people.

Under the same Indian Removal Act, which Jackson pushed through Congress right after taking office, the Georgia state legislature annexed all Cherokee lands in the state and distributed them to whites through a lottery system.[1] Cherokee laws were declared null and void, and Cherokees were no longer permitted to testify against whites in court. The US Supreme Court initially ruled in favor of the government in 1830 but reversed this decision in 1832. "The Cherokee nation, then, is a distinct community, occupying its own territory, with boundaries accurately described in which the laws of Georgia can have no force, and which the citizens of Georgia have no right to enter, but with the assent of the Cherokees themselves, or in conformity with treaties, and with the acts of Congress."[2]

But Jackson had no intention of following the court decision and said so: "John Marshall has rendered his decision; now let him enforce it."[3] The only enforcement in this case was carried out against the Cherokees. In 1835 the remaining members of the tribe were driven out of the southern states and forced on the Trail of Tears to Oklahoma. More than four thousand perished during this relocation enforced by Jackson's government. The other so-called civilized tribes — Creek, Choctaw, Chickasaw, and Seminole — were also driven from their ancestral lands. They were called civilized because they conformed to white culture; some were even slaveholders themselves. But their lands were valuable to people who would make slavery even more profitable, and that meant the Indians had to go.

Jackson was nothing if not consistent throughout his life. He always acted with the interests of the settler colonial project in mind. On September 21, 1814, Jackson and his group of volunteers were stationed in Mobile, Alabama. He was committed to preventing the British from winning New Orleans during the War of 1812. He issued a proclamation titled "To the Free Colored Inhabitants of Louisiana." Jackson invited free blacks to join the army in their own regiments. He promised them "the same bounty, in money and lands, now received by the white soldiers of the United States, viz., one hundred and twenty-four dollars in money, and one hundred and sixty acres of land."[4]

But the right hand took what the left had given. Jackson assured Louisiana's Governor Claiborne that he enrolled these free people because he feared they would join the British war effort or rise up and attack the white population. "We must be prepared to act with promptness, or Mobile and New Orleans by a sudden attack may be placed in the hands of our enemies, and the negroes stimulated to insurrection and massacre, may deluge our frontier in blood."[5]

Jackson was honored during his lifetime with the naming of Jackson, Mississippi (1821), Jacksonville, Florida (1832), and numerous other locations for his dubious achievements of removing Indians and advancing slavery. His legacy received the ultimate seal of approval when his likeness was placed on the twenty-dollar bill nearly a century after he became president, in 1928. Jacksonian

Democracy was nothing more than slavocracy in action: a means of getting whites who were not among the elites to become powerful and wealthy through the American slaveholding industry, as Jackson had done himself. The nation's story of conquest and genocide is perhaps most fully embodied in the figure of Jackson, and it is a story of the present day: Jackson represents the staunch white nationalist American settler, and he is greatly admired by many. Less than two months after taking office, President Trump traveled to Jackson's home in Nashville, the Hermitage, and laid a wreath at Jackson's tomb, calling him "the people's president."

Despite Jackson's wretched history, the effort to cover up his crimes never ends. A closer look demonstrates how eager historians have been to ignore his obvious white supremacist beliefs.

In 2015 an initiative was started to include women on US currency by 2020 to mark the one hundredth anniversary of female suffrage. A 2016 announcement by the Obama administration's Treasury secretary, Jack Lew, would have had Harriet Tubman's image on the twenty-dollar note alongside that of Jackson, a man whose support of slavery she had suffered from and fought against. Having Tubman on the front and Jackson on the back was a misguided attempt to keep the *génocidaire* in the pantheon while pretending to honor the woman who stole herself and others from the clutches of the slavocracy.[6] In 2017, Trump's Treasury secretary Steven Mnuchin rejected even that plan and refused to commit to adding Tubman to any currency.

In 2016 former senator James Webb of Virginia penned an opinion column in the editorial pages of *The Washington Post*. The ridiculous title, "We Can Celebrate Harriet Tubman Without Disparaging Andrew Jackson,"[7] speaks volumes about how Webb and other Americans try to whitewash history. Harriet Tubman should always be celebrated. Jackson should always be disparaged. Any attempt to do both is a vain effort to reconcile the irreconcilable.

MARTIN VAN BUREN

1837–1841

Martin Van Buren was born in the Hudson Valley of New York into a slaveholding family. His father, Abraham, owned six enslaved people. The future president owned one himself, a man named Tom.[1] Tom managed to escape to Canada in 1821, but in 1822 he was discovered living in Worcester, Massachusetts. Van Buren agreed to sell him to the person who found him for fifty dollars if he could capture him without violence. The buyer could not commit to doing so, and so Van Buren never paid. Tom remained a freeman.

At an 1821 constitutional convention the then state senator Van Buren supported giving the franchise to those few free black men who had a minimum of $250 worth of property. This vote was used against him when he ran for president. To garner southern support, he explicitly denied being an abolitionist. He claimed to think slavery wrong but took the position that tampering with the institution was unconstitutional, declaring himself "the inflexible and uncompromising opponent of any attempt on the part of

Congress to abolish slavery in the District of Columbia against the wishes of the slave holding states, and also with a determination equally decided to resist the slightest interference with it in the States where it exists."[2] This argument was typical at the time and allowed him to be considered anti-slavery without being called an abolitionist.[3] He called slaveholders "sincere friends to the happiness of mankind"[4] and published a pamphlet opposing abolition. He supported efforts to ban abolitionist literature from the mail and the gag rule, which prohibited any debate on slavery from taking place in Congress.

Van Buren was a typical northern Democrat. He bent over backward to mollify the slavocracy. Slavery could not be contained because the slaveholders used every means to make sure that it spread. That is why Van Buren continued the removal of Indian tribes from the Southeast, asserting that it "has been steadily persevered in by every succeeding President, and may be considered the settled policy of the country."[5] Slavery could not thrive if the Southeast remained in the hands of indigenous people. The plan was straightforward: First remove Indians from their land, then secure the plantation economy throughout the Southeast.

In 1839, Van Buren attempted to intervene against the cause of freedom in the case of the *Amistad*. The enslaved people on board the ship had been kidnapped in Africa and taken to Cuba. They seized the ship in an insurrection and attempted to sail home, but they were captured in US waters. The Spanish government demanded the return of the ship and its human property to Cuba, and Van Buren was more than ready to comply, seeking a court order extraditing the mutineers and appealing when a federal district court ruled against extradition.[6] When the Supreme Court ruled that the captives must be freed, as the international slave trade had long since been illegal in the United States, Van Buren prepared to capture the newly freed people secretly and to provide legal counsel to the surviving Spanish sailors.[7] Though this preparation was in vain, Van Buren's stance on the *Amistad* case wasn't surprising. He was a true "doughface" — a name for a pro-slavery northerner. He wouldn't be the last one to become president, either.

WILLIAM HENRY HARRISON

1841

William Henry Harrison served the shortest term in office of any American president: He died just thirty-one days after his inauguration. His speech was long, evidently too long for a cold rainy day, and he died from complications of pneumonia one month later. Harrison lacks any presidential legacy, but he looms large because of his actions prior to taking office. He is a key figure in the history of America's extermination of the Indian population and its attempts to expand slavery to those areas where the indigenous population had been decimated.

Harrison was a Virginian. He was the son of a slaveholding farmer who was among the signers of the Declaration of Independence. Initially a student of medicine at the University of Pennsylvania, he joined the army after his father's death — and it was there that Harrison first gained notoriety.

Early 1800s Ohio, Indiana, Illinois, Michigan, Wisconsin, and northeastern Minnesota constituted the western frontier of the white American settlement. For most white Americans, there was no frontier. Step by step they invaded and occupied every region of the indigenous people's country, "from sea to shining sea."

This region, then known as the Northwest, was where Harrison earned his reputation as a *génocidaire*. He made his career in the so-called Northwest Indian War. He fought at the Battle of Fallen Timbers in 1794 and was a signatory of the 1795 Treaty of Greenville, which forced Indians to cede their lands to American settlement. The land that is present-day Indiana thereafter experienced a significant influx of white settlers.

Harrison was eventually appointed governor of the Indiana Territory, where he tried to legalize slavery in 1805 and in 1807. This was in direct contradiction of Article 6 of the ordinance that brought the territory into being in 1797: "There shall be neither slavery nor involuntary servitude in the said territory, otherwise than in the punishment of crimes whereof the party shall have been duly convicted: Provided, always, that any person escaping into the same, from whom labor or service is lawfully claimed in any one of the original States, such fugitive may be lawfully reclaimed and conveyed to the person claiming his or her labor or service as aforesaid."

But like slaveholders everywhere, he didn't let a small thing like the law get in his way. Besides, the article was not retroactive. The old French settlers had held slaves for years and had no intention of giving them up, and so Harrison tried to build upon the already existing practice.

In 1802, Harrison informed Congress that "a very large majority of the Citizens" wanted to repeal Article 6 and that a convention would be called to formalize that desire. The Vincennes Convention was held on Christmas Day and resulted in a resolution to suspend Article 6 for ten years, pending congressional approval. Congress denied the request, but Harrison didn't give up. It should be noted that Congress's primary focus with respect to territories becoming states was to maintain the balance between the slave and free states. Ending slavery was not their objective.

As governor of Indiana, Harrison adopted from other states legislation that denied legal rights to non-whites and attempted to circumvent anti-slavery sentiment. A law passed on September 20, 1803, denied "negroes, mulattos, and Indians" the right to testify against whites in court. An 1805 law made it legal to bring slaves to Indiana and convert them to indentured servants. Slaves marked an X on a document that made them indentured servants for a specified period of time — or indefinitely. Children inherited their parents' indentured status for a period of at least two years.

White settlement had not yet driven out the indigenous population. But as territorial governor of Indiana, Harrison set out to change that. Accommodationist Indian leaders agreed to sell thousands of acres to the new territory, hoping to save something for their people. Tecumseh and his brother Tenskwatawa then led a confederation of tribes in resistance and attempted to get British support against the Americans. Harrison led his forces against Tenskwatawa in 1811 at what came to be known as the Battle of Tippecanoe, a victory that inspired a song used in Harrison's 1840 presidential campaign, "Tippecanoe and Tyler Too." As the indigenous population was driven out, the 1805 act undermined what had been considered a ban on slavery in the territory.

Harrison was a slaveholder his whole life and is said to have fathered six children with an enslaved woman named Dilsia. One of their descendants was Walter White, who served as chairman of the NAACP from 1931 until his death in 1955.

The attempts to change the Northwest Ordinance anti-slavery provisions failed for the simple reason that there were more non-slaveholding whites than slaveholders. Slaveholding settlers simply went farther west to Missouri and Arkansas, where they faced no legal jeopardy. Those who were not slaveholding went to the northwestern territories precisely to escape the slave powers, whose system diminished their ability to thrive economically.

Harrison was caught in the tangle when he ran for Congress in the neighboring state of Ohio in 1822. Knowing of the free soil anti-slavery sentiment there, he fashioned himself as an abolitionist: "I am accused of being friendly to slavery. From my earliest youth to the present moment, I have been an ardent friend of human liberty. At the age of eighteen, I became a member of an Abolition Society, established at Richmond, Virginia, the object of which was to ameliorate the condition of slaves, and procure their freedom by every legal means."[1]

That statement came back to haunt him during the 1840 presidential election. Political expediency forced him to backpedal and deny the sentiments he had expressed nearly twenty years earlier.

> In answer to the inquiry why I used the word "abolition," in designating a society of which I was a member in Richmond, in the year 1791, instead of the word "humane," which is known to be the one by which the society was really distinguished, all that I can say upon the subject is, that if I did term it an abolition society — a fact which I can hardly believe, for I have not been able to see the paper containing my address to the people of the District in 1822 — it must have been forgetfulness, which might easily happen after a lapse of twenty-one years. At any rate, "abolition" was not understood to mean, in 1822, what it now means.[2]

Like the other early presidents, Harrison expanded US territory, drove the indigenous population from their homelands, and fought to expand slavery. His legacy was forged many years before his very brief presidency. Those actions were significant and helped set the stage for conflict and eventually a civil war.

JOHN TYLER

1841–1845

William Henry Harrison died one month after his inauguration, and John Tyler became the first president to hold office who had not been elected. He became known by the moniker His Accidency.

Tyler's biographical information invariably describes him as coming from an "old" Virginia family. *Old* is a covert way of saying "slaveholding," and the Tylers fit that definition. Tyler never backed away from viewing slavery as a benevolent institution. As a member of Congress he voted against the Missouri Compromise because it established that the federal government could, in fact, regulate slavery. While others in his economic class welcomed the coming of another slave state to the Union, Tyler never considered compromising.

He served only one term as president, but he made good use of his time by completing the annexation of Texas before he left office. He succeeded in part by spreading an obvious lie about British plans to annex the Republic of Texas and turn it into a haven for runaway slaves. The annexation question went through various permutations. Under one plan, it was to be admitted not as one state but as two, one free and one slave. Other proposals called for it to be split into as many as five states, increasing slavocracy representation.

Tyler sought help in making the case for annexation from Senator Robert Walker. Walker was born in Pennsylvania but settled in Mississippi and represented that state. He wisely decided not to make the case for annexation by advocating the expansion of slavery. Instead he wrote a lie, claiming that annexation would result in the end of slavery. He penned a thirty-two-page pamphlet titled *Letter of Mr. Walker, of Mississippi, Relative to the Annexation of Texas.*[1] Walker argued that Texas would be a "safety valve" for the internal colonization of black people who might become a labor force for Mexico and the rest of Central America. He claimed that Texas annexation would eventually empty the United States of black people and make the country all white. His idea appealed to northerners who feared the presence of black people. It helped the slavocracy by covertly assisting their plan to create another slave state.

The Texas annexation was a classic case of a "wink wink" that allowed all parties to lie. Northerners had an out since they were able to pretend that another slave state was not being added to the Union. Southerners went along with the insincere scenario so as to get what they wanted. James Polk's victory in the fall of 1844 was considered a mandate for expansion. When all was said and done, the Texas annexation bill was passed and Tyler signed it into law with only two days left in office. Later, Tyler became a member of the Confederate Congress.

In retrospect Tyler is generally regarded as one of the less influential and less effective presidents. He was not elected and did not campaign for the office himself. Yet annexing Texas was a tremendous political victory, and he ought to be regarded as a president who succeeded in enhancing the worst aspects of American colonization. Texas annexation was a huge victory for the slavocracy

— reason enough for history to not treat Tyler kindly. Presidents are sometimes considered successful if they get what they want, and Tyler got something very important that he desired. Acknowledging that fact is a reminder of American presidents' pro-slavery stance.

JAMES K. POLK

1845–1849

The doctrine of Manifest Destiny expressed the belief that the United States had a right, indeed a duty, to expand its territory across North America. The term was coined by journalist John L. O'Sullivan, who in 1845 advocated for the annexation of the Republic of Texas.[1] Texas had been a Mexican territory until Anglo settlers forcefully broke away in 1836. Despite all their noble protestations about liberty, these settlers wanted to maintain slavery, which Mexico had abolished.

Slavery was again the focus of debate in Texas in 1845. Each time a new state sought admission to the Union, the delicate topic of whether it would be slave or free soil emerged. The election of James K. Polk in 1844 played a pivotal role in future events. Polk had an expansionist mind-set, and because he was a slaveholder he had a clear bias regarding this issue.

Polk was raised in North Carolina and Tennessee. His father was a farmer whose estate included about fifty-three slaves, nine of whom the future president inherited. The future president also inherited twenty-four human beings when his grandfather died, and he purchased cotton plantations in Tennessee and Mississippi. He regularly purchased young people between the ages of twelve and twenty-one to work as his unpaid laborers.

Polk's nomination as the Democratic Party's candidate for president was an explicit effort to increase the power of the southern slavocracy.[2] Polk's offenses began before his election in 1844. As Speaker of the House of Representatives, he was a supporter of the gag rule. Every year abolitionist groups sent petitions urging that slavery be abolished in the nation's capital. These entreaties were apparently too much for the slavocracy's gentle sensibilities. Supporters of the gag rule contended that the framers of the Constitution believed that slavery should never be debated by Congress. The last instance of the rule was not lifted until 1844, the year Polk was elected president.

Polk oversaw the doubling of US territory when Mexico lost 55 percent of its land through the Treaty of Guadalupe Hidalgo, which ended the Mexican-American War in 1848. The states of California, Nevada, Arizona, New Mexico, Utah, and portions of Wyoming and Colorado had all been part of Mexican territory. Westward expansion was dressed up with talk of the Manifest Destiny of a benevolent nation; it was a so-called civilized power that wielded the hammer. Polk and others hoped to expand America's slaveholding into the newly claimed territories stolen from the Native Americans. As with his predecessors, Polk engaged in expansionist tactics that resulted in genocide. As a slaveholder, he has never been called to account fully for his self-interested behavior perpetuating the practice of slavery. In fact, he explicitly avoided public disclosure of his personal slaveholding activities. Just three weeks after the war with Mexico began he wrote to his brother-in-law, who was charged with buying more hands for Polk's Mississippi plantation: "It should not be made public that you are making purchases for me."[3]

While Polk cultivated an image of disinterest, the free soilers publicly opposed expanding slavery into any new territories that might be acquired in a war with Mexico. Congressman David Wilmot of Pennsylvania sponsored legislation known as the Wilmot Proviso shortly after the Mexican War began in 1846. Had it become law, the Wilmot Proviso would have prevented the expansion of slavery into any territory acquired from the war. Wilmot made clear that he had "no morbid sympathy for the slave." He favored snatching Mexican land but only "where the sons of toil, of my own race and own color, can live without the disgrace which association with negro slavery brings upon free labor."[4]

Polk countered with yet another compromise, harking back to 1820. The president suggested that the line of slavery continue at 36°30' latitude, which would allow slaveholding in Southern California, New Mexico, and Arizona while leaving Northern California, Washington, Oregon, Idaho, Utah, and Nevada slavery-free. Ultimately both the compromise and the Wilmot Proviso failed and none of the states acquired in the Mexican war allowed slavery. The slavocracy, having defeated the Wilmot Proviso, would continue their legislative victories the following year with the passage of the 1850 Fugitive Slave Act. Polk, like his predecessors who also supported the expansion of slavery and protection of slavocracy rights, ultimately helped to destroy the institution they sought to preserve. Northern opposition to the Fugitive Slave Act would move the nation closer to war.

ZACHARY TAYLOR

1849–1850

Zachary Taylor served in office for only eighteen months. He was inaugurated on March 5, 1849, and he died on July 9, 1850. Some historians say that eating raw fruit and milk on a hot day killed him; others say that it was cholera; yet others believe that he was poisoned. While this may not matter to the topic at hand, what does matter is that Taylor joined the ranks of presidents who committed genocide. Exterminating Indians ran in his bloodline, and slaveholding was a family business for generations. Manifest Destiny was also part of Taylor's legacy.

Taylor was born in Virginia in 1784 to a family designated as "aristocratic" in a country meant to be a haven from aristocracy. He was a descendant of William Brewster, a leader of Plymouth Colony, where the settler project began. Taylor's second cousin was James Madison. He was also related to Robert E. Lee and his clan.

In the state of Virginia, words like *wealthy* and *aristocrat* were synonymous with slaveholding, and Zachary Taylor was guilty on all counts. His father, Richard Taylor, served in the Revolutionary

War — which, as demonstrated earlier, was motivated in large part by a desire by the Americans to maintain slavery and accelerate the stealing of Indian land. He was handsomely rewarded for the effort, receiving a war bonus of six thousand acres of land located in western Virginia in a region that is now the state of Kentucky. In 1790 the elder Taylor owned seven slaves; that number had risen to twenty-six by 1800 and to thirty-seven by 1810.[1]

As an army officer Zachary Taylor rose to the rank of general as he fought the indigenous Sac and Fox Nation in the Black Hawk War and the Seminole tribes in the Florida War, driving them from their lands. He fought in the Mexican War, which reduced that country's territory by half and doubled the size of the United States. Taylor held approximately two hundred people in bondage at the time of his greatest plantation wealth. Over the course of his life he bought and sold others to an unknown degree.

As a plantation owner in Kentucky, Louisiana, and Mississippi, Taylor left his children a great fortune — one gained at the expense of chattel slaves. He always complained that business was bad, that floods washed away his crops, and that he never made as much money as he wanted. Known as "Old Rough and Ready" for his success in killing and relocating Seminoles, he returned to the United States in 1847 intending to continue making a fortune from his unpaid laborers.

In 1840 he purchased the Cypress Grove Plantation, a 1,923-acre tract of land located in Jefferson County, Mississippi. The price of ninety-five thousand dollars — sixty thousand in cash and thirty-five thousand in notes — was a considerable sum of money for this time. He bought not only land but eighty-one humans as well. Most of that county's people, some 80 percent, were enslaved. At the time of his death in 1850, Taylor owned 127 enslaved people on the plantation. In 1850 only 1,733 slaveholders, roughly one-half of 1 percent of all the slaveholders in the nation, owned more than a hundred people each.

The twelfth president of the United States should be remembered for more than dying unexpectedly. The same authors who provide useful information about the degree of his slaveholding also maintain that his "servants" were "as well treated and their welfare as carefully considered as any in the South. Each slave received fresh milk daily and was issued a pound of meat on an average day."[2] Indians struggling to keep their lands resisted as long as they could, but those same authors call them "savages." Taylor and other presidents are still revered no matter how unsavory their conduct. New Hampshire's *Independent Democrat* quite accurately described Taylor in an 1848 editorial as "one of the greatest slaveholders in the United States" who "raises babies for the markets and makes merchandize of his fellow men! He has a hundred mothers, with or without babies, for sale in the shambles. He furnishes creole virgins for the 'hells' of New Orleans, and riots on the ruins of souls for whom the Man of Sorrows died."[3] This nineteenth-century newspaper does a better job of describing how Taylor made his fortune than do many twentieth- and twenty-first-century biographers.

Taylor is a paradox in that he wanted to keep anti-slavery northerners happy. He was chosen as the Whig nominee to keep southerners happy, but he was not as malleable as the powers that be had hoped. He insisted that California and New Mexico be admitted to the Union directly, skipping the process of becoming territories. This decision made it possible for two new anti-slavery states to be admitted to the Union, but only because Taylor knew that these new territories were unsuitable for large-scale cultivation of sugar and cotton and would never have viable plantation economies. He said as much in a letter to his former son-in-law, Jefferson Davis, who had served under him in the Black Hawk War and would go on to become president of the Confederate states.

This Wilmot question should never have been agitated, nature has so arranged matters as regards the ceded

Territory, which will prevent the existence of Slavery
in any portion of it; for no one while in his senses will
carry his slaves there unless he wishes to get them out of
the reach of some civil process; this proviso was gotten
up with no other object but to array the North against
the South, & I much fear its injurious effects before it
[is] finally disposed of; but I hope for the best.[4]

Slavery lasted in the United States as long as it did because of
compromise between abetting sides: keeping an even number of
slave and free states; banning the discussion of slavery in Congress;
passing fugitive slave laws; and determining at which latitude slavery would begin and end. The country's rulers used many tricks to
keep slavery a viable and profitable institution.

Why are these facts not widely discussed today? The United
States still basks in the glory of a romanticized past. If white people
had the right at the time to kill Indians and take their lands and
turn those lands over to the plantation economy, then they probably harbor related feelings of entitlement today. If the institution
of slavery and its aftermath aren't examined, then objective truths
like the inordinate number of blacks being killed by police won't be
questioned, either. If people like Taylor could steal half of Mexico
and be labeled heroic, then modern-day presidents can invade
nations, change regimes, and kill with mechanized drones and
be considered heroic, too. Today's propaganda differs little from
that of Taylor's era. In fact, it relies on it. If the past is examined
through a microscope, then the present must be as well, and that
would create cognitive dissonance. We may ponder the ubiquity of
white privilege in the twenty-first century, but its existence isn't a
mystery. It is exacerbated when the truth of Zachary Taylor's and
other presidents' roles in maintaining the chattel slavery system is
kept hidden.

13

MILLARD FILLMORE

1850–1853

Millard Fillmore was the vice presidential candidate on the 1848 ticket because his running mate, Zachary Taylor, was a slaveholding southerner. Fillmore was one of a long line of northerners who gave in to the slave owners out of political expediency and his own covertly racist beliefs.

As a newly elected congressman in 1838, Fillmore favored abolishing slavery in the District of Columbia. He voted to allow congressional debate and opposed the annexation of Texas. In 1846 he called the Mexican War a "wild and wicked scheme of foreign conquest" meant to add "another slave territory to the United States."

But as the new president in 1850, Fillmore signed the Fugitive Slave Act into law and said there was no need to amend it in any way to protect free people from being kidnapped and sold in the South. Like fellow northerner John Adams, he feared that the presence of free black people in the country would lead to a slave insurrection like the one that had given Haiti its independence fifty years earlier. He finally said that slavery should end, but only on the condition that black people be repatriated to Africa.

The only good thing about the Fugitive Slave Act of 1850 is that it hastened the beginning of the Civil War and thus the end of slavery. It brought the evil of slavery home to northerners who thought they could escape it. The name of the act is a rather bland description that doesn't tell the story of how it exacerbated tensions between North and South. It was not the first fugitive slave law; that one was dated 1793. Like its predecessor, the new version allowed for fugitives to be recaptured and sent back to their slaveholders. The scope of the 1850 legislation is what made it so vile. Not only did it give slaveholders the right to recapture their human property, but it also forced northerners to assist in committing an act that many of them considered to be criminal. A marshal who did not assist in the capture of a fugitive could be fined up to a thousand dollars. Anyone aiding a fugitive could also be fined a thousand dollars or sentenced to six months in jail. The captured person had no right to trial and could not testify on his or her own behalf.

A portion of Fillmore's 1852 message to Congress was suppressed, but it was saved and lives on as "Mr. Fillmore's Views Relating to Slavery: The Suppressed Portion of the Third Annual Message to Congress, December 6, 1852." In this text Fillmore claims to think slavery an evil, but he concludes that it cannot be abolished and that black people, free and enslaved, should be sent away lest they be exterminated in a race war: "I see no remedy but by colonizing the free blacks, either in Africa or the West Indies, or both. This, it appears to me, is all that Congress can do."[1]

Fillmore was not the last pro-slavery northerner; his immediate successors Franklin Pierce and James Buchanan continued in the same vein of placating the South. Compromise and court cases were ultimately unable to keep the nation from splitting into two and going to war.

14

FRANKLIN PIERCE

1853–1857

Franklin Pierce was among the northern members of the Democratic Party who unquestionably served the slave owners. His secretary of war and close friend was Jefferson Davis, the future president of the Confederate rebellion. The Missouri Compromise of 1820, which was once loved by the slave powers, was cast aside in favor of the 1854 Kansas-Nebraska Act, which Pierce drafted along with Senator Stephen A. Douglas of Illinois. It allowed new states to determine whether they would be soil for the slavocracy based on the concept of popular sovereignty. It upended the doctrine of balance, compromises of the sort that led to the creation of two houses of Congress, one that had an equal number of members per state and the other that gave states representation based on population. Since the Missouri Compromise there had been no new slave states admitted to the Union without another free soil state being admitted as well.

During his four-year term Pierce sought to expand slavery not just in the United States but in the Caribbean and Central America as well. He recognized a renegade government established by William Walker, an outlaw American filibuster — someone who instigates military actions in foreign countries without the official support of the US government, but often with its approval and support — living in Nicaragua. Walker was a Tennessean with a predilection for grandiose scheming who briefly held territory in Mexico before deciding to make himself president of Nicaragua and reinstate slavery, which had been abolished there thirty years earlier.[1]

Walker was eventually undone, but the powerful slavery system was eager for more territory. When he wasn't giving a free hand to Walker and other filibusters, Pierce was trying to obtain other countries. He offered Spain one hundred million dollars to purchase Cuba, but the offer came with a threat of annexation if Spain didn't agree to terms. Cuba was just ninety miles from Florida and had a centuries-old slave-based plantation economy that southerners wanted to make their own. The diplomat Pierce chose for the job was the very undiplomatic Pierre Soule. Soule made no secret of his intentions, killed a French ambassador in a duel, and also killed the plan when it became public.[2]

As war approached, Pierce again wrote to his friend Jefferson Davis in 1860 and spoke of a hope to "overthrow political abolitionism at the polls."[3] This letter was discovered at Davis's home by Union troops and was used to accuse Pierce of disloyalty. The accusation was all too true. Pierce was pro-Confederate and deserved the denunciation.

JAMES BUCHANAN

1857–1861

James Buchanan was a northerner, the only president from the state of Pennsylvania. Yet like his predecessors, he wasn't at all interested in addressing the institution of slavery, stating in his inaugural address, "Most happy will it be for the country when the public mind shall be diverted from this question to others of more pressing and practical importance."[1] In fact, he exemplified the term *doughface*, a reference to a northerner with southern sympathies.

Buchanan proved himself to be the worst doughface of all when the Supreme Court handed down the infamous *Dred Scott v. Sandford* decision on March 6, within days of his taking office. Dred Scott was enslaved to an army doctor who briefly served in the states of Illinois and Wisconsin. After the slaveholder's death, Scott sued for his freedom, claiming that his residence in those states made him a freeman. Lower courts agreed with him, and Justice Robert Grier said that the court would probably decide against Scott, but narrowly, on the issue of his freedom. However,

Buchanan wanted more. He would not have been satisfied with
Dred Scott's continued bondage alone. He hoped that the opposition to slavery would disappear once and for all and that white
northerners would no longer have any say in the question of slavery and its expansion.[2]

While he was still president-elect, Buchanan wrote to Justices
John Catron and Robert Grier, telling the latter, "The great object
of my administration will be if possible to destroy the dangerous
slavery agitation and thus to restore peace to our distracted country."[3] Grier agreed with Buchanan and told him so in a letter. He
stated that he, Justice James Wayne, and Chief Justice Roger Taney
"fully appreciate and concur in your views as to the desirableness
at this time of having an expression of the opinion of the Court
on this troublesome question. With their concurrence, I will give
you in confidence the history of the case before us, with the prob-
able result."[4] The court's decision stated that no black person was
a citizen, whether free or enslaved, and that none had any rights
that a white person had to respect, including the right to bring
suit in court. Buchanan had actively and unethically colluded
with the federal judiciary in violation of the law; when the law
became inconvenient it was tossed aside. Buchanan got his wish
in the *Scott v. Sandford* decision. Not only did the 7–2 result strip
all black Americans of their rights as citizens, but it also ruled that
the Missouri Compromise of 1820 was unconstitutional because it
gave the federal government jurisdiction over the question of slavery. The decision was not just the result of evil intent on the part
of seven of the nine Supreme Court justices. It was an attempt to
remove any legal process that could end slavery.

In his attempt to kill the abolitionist movement, Buchanan only
strengthened it and buoyed the endless greed of the slave owners.
Buchanan won the battle in the *Scott v. Sandford* decision, but he
emboldened the movement that would cost his pro-slavery brethren a war eight years later.

1862–1901

RECONSTRUCTION

1865: Nearly two hundred thousand black people serve as United States Colored Troops (USCT) in the Civil War.

1865: The Thirteenth Amendment abolishes slavery but makes an exception for imprisonment.

1866: Frederick Douglass leads a delegation petitioning for a federal law ensuring the vote for African Americans, which Andrew Johnson rejects.

1868: Louisiana votes to send John W. Menard, a black man, to Congress, but he is barred from taking his seat by white members of Congress.

1870: The Fifteenth Amendment to the Constitution allows black men to vote.

1900: The number of black people in the United States has doubled in the past four decades and now stands at 8.8 million.

1900: The average life expectancy for black people is thirty-three years; for white people, it is forty-seven.

ABRAHAM LINCOLN

1861–1865

Abraham Lincoln was long credited with being the "great emanci-pator" and the anti-slavery president. He was in fact quite openly racist and often expressed the belief in keeping America a nation of, by, and for white people. On December 31, 1862, he signed an agreement with one Bernard Kock to take 435 black so-called contrabands to Île à Vache, a satellite island off the coast of Haiti.[1] The next day Lincoln signed the Emancipation Proclamation, but the fact that he had also negotiated a colonization scheme, which he had likely intended to accompany and complement the procla-mation, is largely unknown.

Lincoln is a quintessential American hero. Much of the mythol-ogy surrounding him is worse than sympathetic exaggeration. Lincoln lore is mostly made up of lies. One of his most outspo-ken detractors was radical abolitionist Wendell Phillips. Lincoln's continued advocacy of colonization, the forced migration of black people out of the country, inspired Phillips to call him "a first rate, second rate man." Lincoln was a consummate politician: He had to be dragged kicking and screaming to fight a war to end slavery and ultimately went to war only to save the Union. The Republican Party was founded to prevent the spread of slavery into the western territories, not necessarily to abolish it. Abraham Lincoln made it quite clear that he had no intention of ending slavery where it already existed. Yet his attempt to continue the compromises of the previous hundred years were not enough to keep the slavocracy mollified. They struck first — by Lincoln's design, to attract public support for the Union as defender rather than aggressor — at Fort Sumter, South Carolina, in 1861.

Lincoln is often remembered as the man who personally prosecuted the war and insisted on the defeat of the Confederacy. It is true that he sat by the telegraph and eagerly awaited news of battles. He did fire underperforming generals and lament when they didn't pursue the Confederates. But he would have done none of those things if the Confederates hadn't rebuffed his efforts to compensate them in exchange for their freed slaves or if he hadn't reneged on his promise not to tamper with the institution where it existed.

Most important, he would never have finally waged a war of abolition if the enslaved themselves had not forced him to do so. On May 23, 1861, three enslaved men, Shepard Mallory, Frank Baker, and James Townsend, rowed across the James River in Virginia into Union-held territory at Fort Monroe. Despite federal policy, which required that they be returned to their slaveholder, General Benjamin Butler decided to keep them as contraband of war. The Lincoln administration chose not to punish Butler, and in the ensuing weeks more runaways turned up at Fort Monroe. Within a month five hundred men, women, and children had taken refuge there.[2]

As the war dragged on, the enslaved began freeing themselves wherever Union forces appeared. While northerners debated whether the war was being fought over slavery, the enslaved answered in the affirmative and declared that there was no turning back. There could be no more waffling about whether the Union should maintain slavery. The Union could only be restored without slavery, and the North would have to defeat the South militarily to do it.

Phillips made clear that if it could be said that Lincoln had grown, it was because "we watered him." He was "watered" by Confederate intransigence and the determination of the enslaved to become free. Lincoln is remembered as a martyr in large part because he was assassinated immediately after the war ended. It is easy to see him as heroic precisely because of how he was killed.

In support of the Fugitive Slave Law, Lincoln stated, "We are under a legal obligation to catch and return the runaway slaves. I confess I hate to see them hunted down and carried back to their stripes and unrequited toil, but I bite my lips and keep quiet." Phillips again responded, calling Lincoln the "slave hound of Illinois."[3] Lincoln told black people to their faces that they should leave the country and blamed them and their presence for the Civil War.[4]

Lincoln never gave up his dream of colonization, a dream of fulfilling the settler colonial project and making America a nation for Anglo-Saxons. He established an office to promote colonization within the Interior Department and hired the Reverend James Mitchell to develop a colonization plan, naming him the US commissioner of Negro colonization. One colony nearly came to fruition in the Chiriqui region of Panama until Central American governments protested. Mitchell wrote Lincoln the "Letter on the Relation of the White and African Races in the United States: Showing the Necessity of the Colonization of the Latter."[5] Mitchell didn't mince words, encouraging the president on the first of twenty-eight pages "to produce the separation of those races, the removal of the colored race to a proper locality, and establishment in independence there."

On August 14, 1862, Lincoln met with a group of five black pastors selected by Mitchell and told them that he wanted them and their people out of the country: "But for your race among us there could not be war, although many men engaged on either side do not care for you one way or the other. Nevertheless, I repeat, without the institution of Slavery and the colored race as a basis, the war could not have an existence."[6]

This determination to carry out a plan of ethnic cleansing had very dangerous repercussions for black people, who lived a precarious existence whether or not they were enslaved or free. At the time of Lincoln's meeting with the "intelligent colored men," a wave of violence was falling upon black communities around the country. On August 6, 1862, the *New-York Tribune* reported that violence "commenced weeks ago in Cincinnati, Evansville, Ind., and Toledo." In Brooklyn a mob attacked black workers at a tobacco factory and attempted to burn it down, with the workers inside.

Lincoln was nothing if not consistent. After his meeting with black leaders, after violent attacks on black people, he continued to link emancipation to colonization. On September 23, 1862, he met with his cabinet to discuss a preliminary Emancipation Proclamation and made clear his determination to send black people out of the country. Secretary of the Navy Gideon Welles reported on the meeting: "This was a part of the president's scheme, and had occupied his mind some time before the project for emancipation was adopted, although the historians, biographers, and commentators have made slight, if any, allusion to it. The President, however, and a portion of his Cabinet considered them inseparable, and that deportation should accompany and be part of the emancipation movement."[7]

Not only was emancipation tied to colonization, but so was compensation to the slaveholders, which Lincoln proposed in his congressional address of December 1, 1862, while giving them until January 1, 1900, to complete the process of emancipation. So dedicated are historians to whitewashing history that they lie about evidence that is quite easy to find. Benjamin Butler's account of being asked to develop yet another colonization plan just days before Lincoln's assassination is continually called into question.[8] Anyone questioning whether Lincoln was the "great emancipator" is rebuffed. He may have said in his second inaugural address in March 1865: "If God wills that [the Civil War] continue until all the wealth piled on the bondsman's two hundred and fifty years of unrequited toil shall be sunk, and until every drop of blood drawn with the lash shall be paid by another drawn with the sword."[9] But it was the insistence of the slaves and former slaves themselves, of radical abolitionists, and of intransigent Confederates that forced him to utter such words shortly before he died. It is imperative that we debunk the myth that Lincoln acted initially out of a motivation to help black people — spreading and continuing these falsehoods makes the study of history a sham and keeps Americans uninformed about their past and their present.

ANDREW JOHNSON

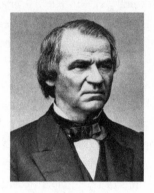

1865–1869

Andrew Johnson was a Tennessee senator who tried to keep his state from seceding along with the rest of the South after Abraham Lincoln's election in 1860. His motivation clearly was not to end slavery, as he owned eight human beings himself. He railed against the power of the slave-owning "aristocrats," but when he replaced Lincoln's first vice president, Hannibal Hamlin, in 1865 and then became president after Lincoln's assassination, he made it clear that he believed in government of, for, and by white people.

Johnson had his own presidential ambitions and had hoped to be the Democratic Party candidate in 1860. Stephen Douglas won that contest, but Johnson did his best to promote southern slaveholding interests despite his loss. He argued to his fellow southerners that they might be able to keep Lincoln in check should he attempt to do more than stop the spread of slavery. His plea for unity was an effort to keep the slavocracy on top in American politics. He knew that secession would mean the end of slavery. He ended up having to flee from his state, but as the only southerner to keep his congressional seat after secession, he put himself in a powerful position in the Lincoln administration.

Lincoln appointed Johnson as military governor of Tennessee in 1862. Johnson seemed to continue his pro-Union efforts as he demanded loyalty oaths from local officials and shut down newspapers supportive of the Confederacy. But he also allowed slaveholders to search contraband camps for their runaway property. He even refused to provide tents or other shelter in the contraband camps in the winter of 1863.[1] He asked Lincoln to exempt Tennessee from the Emancipation Proclamation, and the president agreed, leaving black people enslaved in a state that was mostly in Union hands. He eventually had to take steps toward emancipation, but, in so doing, he managed to get compensation for Union slaveholders in the amount of three hundred dollars for every manumitted man who signed up for service.[2]

The nature of Johnson's wartime relationship with black people played out again after Lincoln's assassination delivered him into the presidency. The Freedmen's Bureau bill of 1865 called for providing lots of forty acres each for rent and eventual purchase by the newly freed people. When Union generals William Sherman and Oliver Howard sought to act on the Freedmen's Bureau legislation by confiscating property abandoned by Confederates to provide for the formerly enslaved, Johnson voided all of these proposals.[3]

Frederick Douglass was correct when he said, "Whatever Andrew Johnson may be, he certainly is no friend of our race."[4] On February 7, 1866, Douglass led a delegation from the Convention of Colored Men to meet with Johnson. Their goal was to secure a commitment to give black men the vote and legal protection to exercise it. In response, the president bragged about being a slaveholder and claimed to have made great personal sacrifices for the people he owned. He expressed concern about poor whites who he believed suffered while blacks were free, and he ended the meeting by suggesting that black people leave the country.[5]

His constant undermining of Reconstruction became too much for the Radical Republicans to bear, and Johnson faced impeachment in 1867. The vote failed to get the two-thirds majority needed to remove him, and he served out the remainder of his term in office. During that time he set the stage for the battle against true emancipation, eviscerating Reconstruction policies wherever he had the chance. Johnson vetoed a Freedman's Bureau bill and a Civil Rights Act and returned confiscated land to former slaveholders.[6]

Americans hungry for hypotheticals should not be asking what would have happened had Lincoln dodged the assassin's bullet. Instead they should wonder what would have happened if his successor had been a true champion of human rights. Lincoln's survival might have meant colonization for four million people. They were emancipated despite his original objectives at the Civil War's outset. Emancipation might have been more meaningful and more effective if Johnson had not been so much like the man who had chosen him as vice president with respect to his attitudes toward black Americans.

ULYSSES S. GRANT

1869–1877

The man who came to be known as Ulysses S. Grant was born Hiram Ulysses Grant to a staunchly abolitionist father, Jesse Root Grant. The elder Grant for a time lived as an apprentice in the home of the tanner Owen Brown in Deerfield, Ohio. Owen Brown was the father of John Brown, the man whose attempt to spark a slave uprising at Harpers Ferry led to the Civil War and indeed the end of slavery.

Jesse Grant's anti-slavery sentiments were well known, but his son Ulysses married into a Missouri slaveholding family shortly after his graduation from West Point. Once he was mustered out of the army in 1853, Ulysses lived among his in-laws and promptly forgot his abolitionist upbringing. According to the manumission papers of the man William Jones, Grant ignored his upbringing further by entering the slaveholding business himself.[1] Grant made up for the sin of holding humans in bondage by waging total warfare and ending the practice once and for all with the military defeat of the slavocracy. It was war that ended slavery, not abolitionist opinion or Lincoln's oratory.

Despite being raised by an abolitionist, Grant voted in 1856 for pro-slavery Democrat James Buchanan over John Fremont, the Republican whose little-known Fremont Emancipation would free slaves under Union army control before Abraham Lincoln issued the better-known Emancipation Proclamation. In 1860, Grant was not yet eligible to vote in Illinois, his new state of residence, but he favored Democrat Stephen Douglas over Abraham Lincoln. Grant's attitudes typified those of many white Americans in the North. They may have been anti-slavery, but only because it was out of sight and out of their minds. If given the opportunity to profit from free labor, they would likely act as Grant did. However, Grant's father would have none of it and refused to help his son when he struggled financially. "When you are ready to come North I will give you a start, but so long as you make your home among a tribe of slaveholders I will do nothing."²

Grant rose from failure at farming and in a variety of business ventures to redeem himself in his return to the army during the Civil War. He chose to "side with patriots over traitors," but like his commander in chief, Abraham Lincoln, he was more concerned with saving the Union than with bringing about emancipation.

Confederate commander Robert E. Lee may have surrendered to Grant in April 1865, but the Confederacy refused to die. After his election and inauguration in 1869, Grant's efforts to protect Reconstruction met with mixed results. He supported legislation that gave him the right to declare martial law and suspend habeas corpus. He established the Justice Department in 1870 to help enforce Reconstruction-era protections of the newly freed population. The success of Reconstruction was always in question, as white southerners did not take their defeat lying down and white northerners inevitably grew tired of fighting for black people. The white revanchists knew that Grant and the rest of white America had no interest in keeping up the fight for black people's human rights in the long term.

Grant was the first post–Civil War president to make the claim that he supported legal rights for black people, yet he contradicted himself in opposing what became known as social equality. Denunciation of the term was kin to supporting segregation, and Grant made clear where he stood during his second inaugural address in 1873: "Social equality is not a subject to be legislated upon, nor shall I ask that anything be done to advance the social status of the colored man, except to give him a fair chance to develop what there is good in him."[3]

Atrocities such as the 1873 massacre in Colfax, Louisiana, in which more than one hundred black men were killed on Easter Sunday by a mob of whites determined to oust Republican officials, proved this to be true. Only nine of the ninety-seven men indicted were put on trial, and only three were convicted. Their convictions were overturned in an 1876 Supreme Court case, *United States v. Cruikshank*. The court ruled that the Enforcement Acts used to protect black voting rights applied only to "state actors" and not to individuals. Whites who opposed Reconstruction knew that they had only to continue committing acts of terror in order to overthrow the small amount of progress made by black people.

The Colfax Massacre was widely denounced, but the culprits were never punished. As was often the case in Reconstruction-era atrocities, they managed to avoid jail even when apprehended. Grant left office under a cloud of scandal over actions carried out by political cronies. The bigger scandal was the end of what was left of the feeble federal effort to protect black people from terrorism. Rutherford B. Hayes was the beneficiary of Grant's languor.

RUTHERFORD B. HAYES

1877–1881

Rutherford B. Hayes has gone down in history as "Rutherfraud" because of the scandalous way in which he attained the presidency. The Republican Hayes lost the popular vote to Democrat Samuel Tilden in 1876. Southern Democrats questioned the eligibility of black voters in Florida, South Carolina, and Louisiana as part of an ultimately successful plan to undermine Reconstruction. A fifteen-member commission of senators, congressmen, and Supreme Court justices finally ruled in Hayes's favor, but not without getting a promise to end once and for all the faltering federal commitment to Reconstruction.

The Republican Party was considered the port while all else was the storm, but in the 1876 election both parties were equally bad. White southerners were relentless in their quest to nullify the limited black political power that had emerged after the Civil War, and the Republican Party wanted to move away from working to defend the rights of the newly freed people.

Reconstruction hung by a thread when the wheeling and dealing began to determine the winner of the 1876 presidential election. Hayes's victory was not made official until March 2, 1877, just two days before the inauguration was to take place. On April 20, 1877, Hayes ordered the reposting of the last remnants of federal troops who were stationed in South Carolina and Louisiana. Reconstruction had already been killed by a Democratically controlled Congress, which would not appropriate funds to uphold the Enforcement Acts designed to ensure black enfranchisement. In any case, the departure of the last federal troops effectively ended the last voting rights protections.

Hayes had a career as a Union army officer and claimed to care for the "poor colored people of the south." But he betrayed those values because of ambition and political expediency. The press and most politicians had readily accepted the canard that Reconstruction was a failure that allowed corrupt and incompetent black men to hold office. Tales of northern carpetbaggers and their southern scalawag allies were accepted as true. A bloody war and twelve years of a guerrilla campaign had worn down what little resolve existed among white northerners. So great was the bitterness and fear that many southern blacks spoke openly of leaving the Republican Party, but political leaders spoke out against confronting Hayes. John Langston, president of Howard University, declared that he had "received from his [Hayes's] own lips the most positive assurances that it was the purpose of his Administration to secure by any and every legitimate means within its power and control, our protection, promotion and recognition."[1]

The Hayes administration was just the latest disaster to befall black people since the start of the Civil War. Lincoln had been forced to fight for emancipation every time an enslaved person escaped to Union lines. Andrew Johnson had wanted no part of Reconstruction and was only prevented from undoing the Fourteenth and Fifteenth Amendments by the continued commitment of white Republican northerners. Grant was supposed to be the president who would realize justice and equality for the newly freed people, but he had failed to fight effectively against those promoting the return of legalized white supremacy. By the time Hayes ran for president, the die was cast against black people. They were literally outnumbered and outgunned; the hope and joy they had felt at emancipation proved to be illusory. The constant effort to find a friend between the two dominant political parties began its ignominious tradition, which continues into the present day.

Having made his deal with the devil to gain the presidency, Hayes did little while in office except veto legislation passed by the Democratic majority in Congress. In the winter of 1878–1879, the persistent violence exacted against black people in the former Confederate states created a great exodus to Kansas. Called the Exodusters, as many as forty thousand people fled their homes in search of protection from mob rule. This process did nothing to inspire Hayes to action. Instead he wrote in his diary on May 25, 1879: "The exodus of colored people from the South still attracts attention. The effect is altogether favorable. The tendency will be to force the better class of Southern people to suppress the violence of the ruffian class, and to protect the colored people in their rights. Let the emigrants be scattered throughout the Northwest; let them be encouraged to get homes and settled employment."[2]

Hayes wrote this nonsense in his diary, so it is safe to assume that he really believed it. Or perhaps it was wishful thinking, meant to exculpate his guilt at having thrown the last bit of justice out the window to secure his political fortunes. In any case, he lived up to the nickname Rutherfraud and began a long line of presidential betrayal.

JAMES A. GARFIELD

1881

James Garfield had served as president for only four months when an assassin shot him in July 1881. He came to the office after a long history of public service as an Ohio state legislator, a member of Congress, a Union army brigadier general in the Civil War, and a US senator. In all of these roles he impacted the lives of black people, and so we can assess him and his beliefs through them, his limited time in the Oval Office notwithstanding.

The usual defense of racism is to excuse an individual by claiming that he was a "man of his times." This description certainly fits Garfield. As a young man he wrote, "The simple relation of master and slave was not unchristian."[1] He referred to himself as being anti-slavery but abjured abolition, saying it was representative of an "overheated and brainless faction."[2] The same man who supported arming blacks in the war as soldiers said, "But it is not in my heart to lay a feather's weight in the way of our Black Americans if they choose to strike for what was always their own."[3] Those words meant little when he had the wherewithal to protect black citizenship rights. He became an advocate for states' rights at the expense of black southerners' rights to vote and to live without fear of white terrorism.

These inconsistencies defined Garfield as a "man of his times." His attitudes were not uncommon for a white northerner, first being anti-slavery, then fighting for the Union and perhaps expressing opposition to slavery, but ultimately putting white people first. The same man who spoke up for the rights of black soldiers felt "repugnance" at the idea of their having voting rights. He expressed the desire to send them all away, as he never "learned to love them."[4]

Garfield was similar to Lincoln in that he never gave up his dream of an America without black people. He may not have served as president for very long, but he typified the office's relationship with black America. Every presidential election in the post–Civil War era produced uncertainty and angst over which candidate would be better for black people. Frederick Douglass said, "We must have Garfield," only to find himself out of a job when the man he endorsed appointed someone else to his position as marshal of the District of Columbia. Douglass didn't go quietly; he asserted, "Whatever may be the ostensible reasons given for it, the real ground of opposition to me is that I am a colored man, and that my sympathies are with my recently enslaved people."[5] The ensuing controversy forced Garfield to appoint Douglass to the position of recorder of deeds.

Douglass was to be disappointed again and again. The post-emancipation period was an endless loop of betrayals as Douglass and other black leaders strove to keep their worst enemies at bay. But Democrats and Republicans were far more concerned about competing to be seen as the white people's party than they were about cultivating support among blacks. Garfield's actions during his brief tenure typified those of his successors.

CHESTER A. ARTHUR

1881–1885

Chester Arthur was Garfield's vice president and came to office after his assassination. Raised by a staunchly abolitionist father, as a young attorney he took on two landmark cases that established legal rights for black people. In the Lemmon Slave Case he argued that eight enslaved people brought to New York State were automatically freed once they arrived. Then in 1856 he argued on behalf of Lizzie Jenkins, a black woman expelled from horse-car public transportation.[1]

But Arthur came to political power when segregation was ascendant. The Jim Crow system that would reign for nearly one hundred years emerged during his time in office. While Republican presidents Grant, Hayes, and Garfield each did less and less for black southerners and diminished federal efforts on their behalf, Arthur was a Stalwart, a faction within the Republican Party that was willing to accommodate the South and many of whose members came from Confederate states. In 1883 the Supreme Court declared that the Enforcement Act, the Civil

Rights Act of 1875, was unconstitutional. The act had guaranteed public accommodation and prohibited exclusion from jury service. The court ruled that the federal government did not have jurisdiction over private entities, which were therefore allowed to discriminate. Republicans in Congress introduced five different bills in an effort to replace the Civil Rights Act, but they all failed in the absence of presidential pressure.[2] In his annual message to Congress in 1883, Arthur mentioned the end of the Civil Rights Act in the very last paragraph. He blandly and untruthfully stated that new legislation would receive his "unhesitating approval."[3]

While Arthur certainly did hesitate to fight for the rights of black people, he was eager to criticize the victims. He admonished one Georgia leader: "You proved yourselves incapable of holding those States when they were placed boldly in your grasp." On other occasions he stated that blacks "do not help the party as much as white officials" and "excel in office begging."[4]

There was no hesitation in the black community in condemning presidential inaction. Charles Hendley, then editor of the *Huntsville (Alabama) Gazette*, put it poignantly and presciently: "Spit upon in the house of his friends, despised and ignored at feast times, and recognized only when his services are needed — is the lot of the negro."[5]

GROVER CLEVELAND

1885–1889

In 1884, Grover Cleveland became the first Democrat elected president since the end of James Buchanan's term, twenty-four years earlier. Although he was a northerner and governor of New York, white southerners broke out in spontaneous celebration. The Georgia state legislature even halted its session in order to join one of those festivities.[1]

The reaction to the election of a Democrat typified this period, the nadir of black political power post-emancipation. The hopes of the emancipation era were dashed when the South reasserted itself and the North equivocated in its defense of black citizens. Black people had repeatedly supported Republicans for president only to be disappointed when they did little or nothing to stop the ascendancy of the Jim Crow era. In the case of Cleveland, there was a desperate need to believe that he would not live up to the adulation accorded him by white southerners.

Cleveland himself gave black people reason to fear. The Republican Party's support of a civil rights act was used against them. Dubbed the

Force Bill by opponents, its defeat became a rallying cry and a slogan in the Cleveland campaign. "No Force Bill! No Negro Domination in the South!" was a far more effective talking point than tariffs or other issues said to be of concern to voters. Cleveland asserted that the proposed legislation "especially menaces the welfare and prosperity of the South" and called it "a most atrocious measure."[2]

T. Thomas Fortune, editor and owner of one of the nation's leading black-owned newspapers, *The New York Globe*, sought mostly in vain to reassure his readers that they had nothing to fear from a Cleveland presidency. His editorial "Colored Men Keep Cool" was written in November 1884 as an effort to stem the panic that ensued after the election: "There is no power, nor do we believe there is any inclination, in the Democratic party to tamper with any fundamental right conferred upon us by the Federal constitution."[3]

In his inauguration speech Cleveland attempted to assuage fears, saying of blacks that "all discussion as to their fitness for the place accorded to them as American citizens is idle and unprofitable except as it suggests the necessity for their improvement." Cleveland's words were less than reassuring, and his subsequent acts appointing southern segregationists to high office were downright alarming. Two southern segregationists joined his cabinet: Lucius Q. C. Lamar of Mississippi as secretary of the interior, and Augustus H. Garland of Arkansas as attorney general.

The black political response to Cleveland differed little from what had been offered up after emancipation: wishful thinking; predictable, feigned expressions of shock; and pleas for mercy from the merciless.

Despite Frederick Douglass's words of support, Cleveland asked for his resignation as recorder of deeds. The new president continued the practice of appointing black ambassadors to Liberia and Haiti, but he did nothing to end lynch law, by which means black people were killed without due process or repercussion, or the continued attacks on what was left of Reconstruction.

Frederick Douglass was not the only black person in this dilemma. The race lived in states of fear broken by short periods of hope for political salvation. Cleveland would return to office later and continue his work as the president of the white segregationist party.

BENJAMIN HARRISON

1889–1893

Benjamin Harrison was the grandson of William Henry Harrison, the thirty-one-day president. He was also a Republican, and that meant that his election was the cause of great optimism among black people.

Harrison's personal history gave some legitimacy to the wishful thinking. During the Civil War, General Benjamin Harrison defended the federal government in an 1864 lawsuit brought by Confederate sympathizers who had been imprisoned by the Union army. He directly addressed the racism that was wrought by the chattel slavery system: "One of the meanest things in this whole world order, one of the meanest political sentiments it ever uttered, was its constant expression of hatred of the negroes."[1]

These comments were not an isolated incident of language deployed to win a court case. When the Civil Rights Act of 1875 was overturned by the Supreme Court on October 15, 1883, Harrison spoke eight days later to a group of "colored citizens": "There has never been a proposition looking to the striking off of a shackle from the black man's wrist, or from his mind or from his personal freedom which has not received my hearty endorsement and my personal help — not one."[2] During his 1888 campaign against then president Cleveland he reiterated his support of the franchise: "I feel very strongly upon the question of a free ballot . . . I would not be willing to purchase the Presidency for a compact of silence upon this question."[3]

But Harrison was less than enthusiastic about protecting the rights of black Americans after he assumed office. Once again black Republicans received only a few token appointments. When Harrison met with southern white Republicans he assured them that they needn't worry about the end of slavery.

The Federal Elections Bill of 1890 had the appearance of legislation that could pass in the Republican-controlled Congress. It called for federal oversight of elections in cities with more than twenty thousand people, any congressional district where more than one hundred voters requested this supervision, and counties or parishes upon the application of fifty voters.[4] This was essentially the same measure that Grover Cleveland had campaigned against, the so-called Force Bill. It would have applied to the whole country, but it was logically understood to be needed most in the southern states. The House passed the bill, but the Senate never took action.

Democrats retook control of the House in 1890, and, in April 1891, Harrison responded by making a pilgrimage to the South with cabinet members and his family in tow. Memphis, Tennessee, mayor Lucas Clapp made it clear who was in charge when he said in his introduction of the president that there was a "paramount aim and purpose with us to guard our social purity, preserve our civilization and maintain Caucasian prestige and supremacy." The president said nothing in response. He went on to discuss the theme of his trip: that majority rule held sway in American law. He was telling white southerners to forget about efforts to make them follow the Fourteenth and Fifteenth Amendments of the Constitution. They could do as they wished. Like other Republican presidents at the end of nineteenth century, Harrison wanted to get white southern votes, and that meant that black people and their political needs had to be ignored. Harrison made no effort to pass the Federal Elections Bill, and the lack of presidential imperative led to its inevitable death.

GROVER CLEVELAND

1893–1897

The presidential election of 1892 presented a repeat of the Benjamin Harrison–Grover Cleveland rivalry, with Cleveland winning a second term. Cleveland made it clear that he would live up to the reputation of the Democrats as the white people's party. He spoke against the already defeated Federal Elections Bill, the so-called Force Bill. The Democratic Party platform bizarrely claimed that it would "injure the colored citizen more than the white" and that it would lead to "the subjugation of the colored race to the control of the party in power, and the reviving of race antagonisms, now happily abated."[1]

The Democrats controlled the White House and both houses of Congress. The lesson that Republicans took from the overwhelming defeat was that white America either wanted to actively deprive blacks of all human and citizenship rights or, at a minimum, didn't want to hear about blacks and their problems.

The Supreme Court handed down its notorious *Plessy v. Ferguson* decision during Cleveland's second term. The court ruled by a vote of 8–1 that discrimination was constitutional and not a violation of the Fourteenth Amendment. Cleveland said nothing after this decision was made in May 1896 but had readily spoken up when a black man made the same case the previous fall.

On September 18, 1895, Booker T. Washington gave his famous Atlanta Compromise speech in which he made the case for black accommodation to white rule in exchange for work and education: "The wisest among my race understand that the agitation of questions of social equality is the extremist folly." The compromise made him the king of black patronage, the gatekeeper for black aspirations.

Cleveland agreed with Washington wholeheartedly and told him so effusively: "Your words cannot fail to delight and encourage all who wish well for the race. And if your colored fellow-citizens do not favor your utterances, gather new hope and form new determination to gain every valuable advantage offered them by their citizenship, it will be strange indeed."[2]

After Cleveland left office, he and Washington reunited in New York on April 14, 1903, at the Southern Education Association dinner. Andrew Carnegie was present, as were other philanthropists and the mayor of New York City. As a quartet from historically black Hampton University sang "Old Black Joe," the former president said these words: "Let us try to be tolerant and considerate of the feelings and even the prejudice or racial instinct of our white fellow-countrymen of the South, who, in the solution of the negro problem must, amid their own surroundings, bear the heat of the day and stagger under the weight of the white man's burden."[3]

Cleveland had been out of office for seven years, but as the only president to serve two non-consecutive terms, he still had hopes for regaining that office. *The San Francisco Call* reported, "If there had been any doubt that Grover Cleveland has third term aspirations that doubt was dispelled to-night, when the former President made a palpable bid for Southern support." Cleveland was never president again, but the script for winning that office has changed little since that time.

— 25 —

WILLIAM MCKINLEY

1897–1901

William McKinley seemed to have all the credentials needed to enjoy support from black Americans. He was a Republican born into an abolitionist family in Ohio. As a young man he fought for the Union in the Civil War. He came of age as a politician who spoke in defense of black voting rights and promised to protect them. However, he was still a white American man dependent upon other white men for success in politics. When he had the chance to avoid an imperial war against Spain, he didn't. When he could have protected the lives of black people in his own country, he didn't do that, either.

By the end of the nineteenth century, the surviving indigenous people had been conquered and almost all of their lands had been stolen. African Americans were freed from chattel slavery only to live a day-to-day existence in fear of mob violence. Manifest Destiny was still the order of the day, as was the Monroe Doctrine and its claim that only the United States would control North America. There were numerous efforts to expand slavery by invading and annexing Cuba as a state. The Spanish wanted to keep what was left of their once-vast empire and had no intention of giving it or any other colonies away. The Cuban people wanted independence, as did Puerto Ricans. In the Pacific, Filipinos and the Mahos of Guahan, called Guam by the Spanish, also wanted theirs. These struggles for independence created an opportunity for the United States to steal these territories from Spain and control them for itself. Anti-Spanish propaganda was used to gain popular support for an American empire and for denying people the self-determination they had long sought. At the end of the Spanish-American War, Cuba was independent of Spain but dependent on the United States. Puerto Rico, Guam, and the Philippines all became American territories. In a four-month-long war, McKinley had sent the last of the European powers away from America's area of influence in the Western Hemisphere and expanded America's imperial reach all the way to Asia.

It was a watershed year for black Americans, too, and not in a good way. There was debate about the war itself and the question of whether blacks should support it. In a forerunner of debates in decades to come, some believed that black participation in the fighting would lead to respect and freedom from discrimination and oppression. That was the opinion expressed in the *Indianapolis Freeman* newspaper: "It pays to be a little thoughtful . . . The strife [against the Philippines] is no race war. It is quite time for the Negroes to quit claiming kindred with every black face from Hannibal down. Hannibal was no Negro, nor was Aguinaldo [the Filipino nationalist leader]. We are to share in the glories or defeats of our country's wars, that is patriotism pure and simple."[1] In an age when the horrible doctrine of separate but equal was the law of the land, other voices counseled opposition. Ida B. Wells-Barnett didn't hold back: "Negroes should oppose expansion until the government was able to protect the Negro at home."[2]

Blacks fought, but at the end of the day they were no better off than if they had not. In November 1898 one of the last bastions of Reconstruction was violently overthrown in Wilmington, North Carolina. The biracial city council made up of Democrats and Republicans was forced out of office by a mob of armed whites. An estimated sixty black people were killed and more than two thousand were forced to flee for their lives.

Pleas for help from the Republican McKinley administration were unheeded. There was no investigation, no mention of the atrocity from the man who had fought in the war that ended slavery and had received black votes when he ran for the presidency in 1896.

The Democrats were the party of open and proud white supremacy, and Republicans were considered the only reasonable option in the face of lynch law terrorism. This pattern of promising support that never materialized would recur into the twenty-first century. The effort to pass an anti-lynching bill foundered and was equally unsuccessful for the next five decades. Presidents may have sought black votes, but the support of black voters never mattered very much when action was needed to protect their lives.

On September 6, 1901, President McKinley was in Buffalo, New York, at the Pan-American Exposition World's Fair. Leon Czolgosz joined a receiving line as if to greet him, but instead he fired two gunshots at McKinley, who died from his wounds eight days later. The first man to reach Czolgosz was not one of the Secret Service agents tasked with protecting the president. Instead, James Benjamin Parker, a black man originally from Georgia, prevented the assassin from firing a third shot and was the first to wrestle him to the ground. Parker was working at the World's Fair as a waiter and had taken the opportunity to meet the president. However, his very presence may have changed McKinley's fate. According to one story, at least one Secret Service agent was busy looking at the black man instead of observing the crowd as he should have been doing. Parker seized the shooter first and knocked the gun from his hand.

Parker was circumspect about his role in the events of that day but also wanted black people to be credited with his heroics: "I am sorry I did not see him four seconds before. I don't say that I would have thrown myself before the bullets. But I do say that the life of the head of this country is worth more than that of an ordinary citizen and I should have caught the bullets in my body rather than the President should get them. I can't tell you what I would have done and I don't like to have it understood that I want to talk of the matter. That's all any man can do." In the same modest statement, Parker added these words, "I am a Negro, and am glad that the Ethiopian race has whatever credit comes with what I did. If I did anything, the colored people should get the credit."[3]

Black people did exult in Parker's heroism and gave him the highest praise. While McKinley lay wounded but still alive, Booker T. Washington rejoiced that a black man had "saved the president from death."[4] Not only black people but the white press, too, wrote about the "tawny lion of the exposition."[5] One of McKinley's Secret Service agents admitted, "That colored man was quicker than we. He nearly killed the man."

Parker's heroics were quickly forgotten after McKinley died and Czolgosz was put on trial. The same Secret Service agent who credited Parker suddenly denied his existence: "I never saw no colored man in the whole fracas." Having failed in their duty, McKinley's bodyguards were not going to credit a black man who acted when they did not. Parker was not called to testify at the trial and was remembered mainly by other black people who were angry that he was so quickly dismissed and discredited. He made a living as a speaker for mostly black audiences until he succumbed to alcoholism and died in a psychiatric hospital. His unclaimed body was dissected by medical students.[6]

1902–1963

EARLY TWENTIETH CENTURY

1920: With the passage of the Nineteenth Amendment, all black people, men and women, gain the right to vote.

1927: When the Mississippi River floods, thousands of black residents in Mississippi and Arkansas are forced at gunpoint to work in labor camps repairing the levees.

1933: Franklin Roosevelt begins suggesting a national minimum wage, which is permanently established in 1938.

1941–1945: More than one million black Americans serve in the military during World War II.

1947: The percentage of southern black people registered to vote rises to 12 percent, from 3 percent in 1940.

1950: The number of black people in the United States reaches fifteen million.

1950: The average income for a black family is less than 55 percent that of a white family.

1955: Lamar Smith encourages black voters to fill out absentee ballots in Brookhaven, Mississippi, for which he is shot to death.

1955–1956: The Reverend Dr. Martin Luther King, Jr., leads the yearlong Montgomery Bus Boycott.

1957: Nine black students are the first to attend the segregated Central High School in Little Rock, Arkansas.

THEODORE ROOSEVELT

1901–1909

In 1901, Vice President Theodore Roosevelt rose to the presidency upon the assassination of President McKinley. Despite the desperate attachment of black Americans to the Republican Party, Roosevelt was quite openly racist. Before he became president, Roosevelt wrote that black people were "altogether inferior to the whites"[1] and opined that "a perfectly stupid race can never rise to a very high plane; the Negro, for instance, has been kept down as much by lack of intellectual development as by anything else."[2]

Roosevelt's views were shared by most of white America. He also shared a contradictory belief that some black people might rise above their inherent inferiority and prove themselves useful to some extent. At that time the most politically useful was Booker T. Washington. The blessing of the "Wizard of Tuskegee" could lead to a noteworthy job, funding for an organization, or entry into Washington's prodigious list of contacts. In his famous Atlanta Exposition speech of 1895, Washington had made the case for accommodation. He had asked blacks to cease agitating for citizenship rights and an end to segregation. As recompense, powerful white people were kind to Washington and the people he designated as being acceptable. Theodore Roosevelt would surely find some use for such an egregiously opportunistic black man, who even claimed to see something positive in the increased number of reports of lynching: "It seems to indicate a going backward rather than a going forward. It really indicates progress. There can be no progress without friction."[3]

Yet a seemingly innocuous event set off a firestorm for both men. On October 16, 1901, Booker T. Washington dined with the president and his family. A reporter noted Washington's name in a guest book and a presidential secretary confirmed: "Booker T. Washington, of Tuskegee, Alabama, dined with the president last evening."

Reaction was swift and put anti-black race hatred on full public view. *The Richmond Times* raged that Roosevelt advocated "that negroes shall mingle freely with whites in the social circle — that white women may receive attentions from negro men." Mississippi senator James K. Vardaman called Roosevelt a "coon-flavored miscegenationist." South Carolina senator Ben Tillman went straight to the point: "The action of President Roosevelt in entertaining that nigger will necessitate our killing a thousand niggers in the South before they will learn their place again."

Roosevelt was not predisposed to being seen as doing anything favorable to black people after reactions like these. As for Washington, black people defended him because of the new enemies he had made, not because of anything he had done for them. Opponents like William Monroe Trotter didn't stop their criticism of Washington, however. Trotter admonished him for hypocritically advising blacks not to seek social interaction with whites yet accept an opportunity to dine with the most powerful white man in the country.

Shocked by the criticism, Roosevelt and his staff began a desperate damage control effort. Alternately they claimed that

Washington came for a luncheon, not a dinner; confirmed the invitation; and tried to say that Washington was never there at all. Then they claimed that neither Mrs. Roosevelt nor the daughters attended the dinner. Neither man was prepared for the level of vitriol following the meal. Roosevelt later said that reaction to his invitation made him "melancholy" and admitted, "I never thought much about it at the time. It seemed to me so natural & so proper." As someone who acted within the socially acceptable bounds of racism Roosevelt was initially unprepared for the lynch mob lovers but quickly regained his political acumen.

By the time Theodore Roosevelt entered office Republicans had long since abandoned their most loyal constituency, but in the face of legalized segregation and lynch law the Republicans were still seen as black people's best chance. Black northerners were still able to exercise the franchise and Roosevelt knew it. That is why he waited until after election day in 1906 to announce that he was committing a grave injustice against a group of black soldiers.

The Twenty-Fifth Infantry Regiment of "Buffalo Soldiers" — a name for the black regiments of the time — arrived at Fort Brown near Brownsville, Texas, on July 28, 1906. From the moment they appeared, white residents kept up a campaign of vicious harassment and threats. When a white man was shot to death, members of the regiment were forced to flee a mob of people who accused them of committing the murder. Tensions were so high that the regimental commander ordered an early curfew and confined the troops to their barracks. A second shooting was blamed on the already quarantined soldiers despite confirmation of their presence in the fort. Without an official charge or trial, 167 of the troops were dishonorably discharged, deprived of pensions, and prevented from gaining federal employment or reinstatement to the army. This decision was not announced until November 5, 1906, after congressional elections had taken place and leaders such as W. E. B. Du Bois had urged black voters to stay in the Republican column.

Dr. Charles Morris, pastor of New York's Abyssinian Church, spoke for most of black America when he described the chain of events: "The president's decree was signed the day after the election. He shot us when our gun was empty. But we shall have two years to work and our slogan shall be a Republican Congress to protect our people in the South, and a Democratic president to resent the insult heaped upon us. Thus shall we answer Theodore Roosevelt, once enshrined in our love as our Moses, now enshrouded in our scorn as our Judas."[4]

Congressional investigations and an army reappraisal concluded that the 167 discharges were done properly. There was one outspoken white defender of the soldiers, Republican senator Joseph Foraker of Ohio. Roosevelt was apoplectic at the opposition and ignored every request for reconsideration of his decision: "Some of those men were bloody butchers; they ought to be hung . . . It is my business and the business of nobody else. It is not the business of Congress . . . If they pass a resolution to reinstate these men, I will veto it; if they pass it over my veto, I will pay no attention to it. I welcome impeachment."[5]

But Senator Foraker kept fighting on their behalf. He demanded a Senate investigation of Roosevelt's decision and in the process made at least one strange bedfellow. South Carolina senator Ben Tillman, the same man who advised lynching a thousand people to make up for the Washington dinner invitation, sided with Foraker, if only to embarrass Roosevelt. Roosevelt's "inoculation" of black people "with the virus of social equality" made the president "more responsible than the soldiers for this trouble."

Foraker took on Roosevelt publicly. At the 1907 Gridiron Club dinner he insulted Roosevelt to his face over the Brownsville decision.[6] At a time when senators were elected by state legislatures and not by popular vote, Foraker risked and indeed lost his seat in the 1908 election.

Stung by criticism of his handling of the Brownsville case and resurrecting his own biases, Roosevelt dispensed with any doubt that he believed in the most prevalent rationale for hatred of black men. In his 1906 Congressional address, he had stated that rape of white women by black men was the principal cause of lynch mob violence.[7] It is noteworthy not only that Roosevelt had proved his racism with this statement but also that Booker T. Washington still would not express any opposition to the man who threw him under the proverbial bus, did a great injustice to black soldiers, and reinforced reasons used to target black men for race violence. Washington never bit the hand that he hoped might feed him: "Of course you must bear in mind that he has for his object the saying of something that will help to make life and property for the Negro in the South safer, and in order to do this he has, in a measure, placed himself in touch with the Southern people. I am now simply presenting his side of the case."[8]

Washington made clear that he had no intention of jeopardizing his relationship with Roosevelt and acknowledged that the loyalty would prove to be problematic: "The enemy will, as usual, try to blame me for all of this. They can talk; I cannot, without being disloyal to our friend, who I mean to stand by throughout his administration."[9] Two years later he had not changed his mind: "The bulk of the Negro people are more and more inclined to reach the decision that even though the President did go against their wishes in dismissing the soldiers at Brownsville, he has favored them in nine cases out of ten . . . It is not the part of common sense to cherish ill will against one who has helped us in so many ways as the President has."[10] Theodore Roosevelt would not be the last president who received high praise despite expressing and practicing blatant anti-black racism.

WILLIAM HOWARD TAFT

1909–1913

William Howard Taft assumed the presidency after serving as Theodore Roosevelt's secretary of war. When Roosevelt left office, Taft was his handpicked successor. The Republican Party, which had done so little but remained the black people's party, was again in power. They once again proved themselves to be false friends to people desperate for even the appearance of fair treatment.

Taft's Republican predecessors had gone through the motions of protecting black political and human rights in the southern states, but he didn't even bother to pretend. During the 1908 campaign he wrote, "The truth is that the negro question so far as the South is concerned in many of the States is a mere ghost of a past issue . . . and I don't propose to raise it again except in a discussion with the negroes themselves as to their course in the matter."[1] Before he was inaugurated he communicated through Booker T. Washington that he wanted all black appointees removed from their offices in the South. William D. Crum is one such example. Born into freedom in a racially mixed family, he was a physician who became active in South Carolina Republican politics. Theodore Roosevelt had appointed him as collector of customs in Charleston in 1902, but the Senate refused to confirm him. The previous president had used recess appointments to keep him in office, but as president-elect, Taft made it clear that he wanted Crum out before his inauguration.

In a December 1908 speech Taft said the federal government had nothing whatsoever to do with the dreaded "social equality," a code word for full citizenship rights. He also wanted nothing to do with controversies about black officeholders. The presence of a handful of black people appointed to government positions was all the entire group had to show for forty years of supporting Republicans. Taft had decreed that even that hope was gone.

Booker T. Washington may not have held any government position, but he was the go-to black man with whom presidents conferred on any issues impacting black people. As he said himself, he was "most happy" to provide the same assistance to Taft that he did to Roosevelt to "raise the standard of colored people holding office under him." Washington asked Crum to meet him in Philadelphia but first admonished him to tell no one about their meeting. When Crum arrived, he found that Washington had already prepared a letter of resignation. Washington wrote to Emmett Scott, one of his Tuskegee machine right-hand men:

> Mr. Taft positively will not re-nominate him. The only question is, whether he can serve his own interests by getting out gracefully or being forced out. Mr. Taft feels most kindly towards him and is going to do his best to provide him something else, but he will feel more kindly to him if he gets out in the way suggested, that is, by resigning. Further than this, I find that people everywhere, even among our best friends, are tired of the Crum case.[2]

Having sacrificed Crum, Washington went about the business of serving Taft as happily as he had said he would.

Washington quite shamefully took credit for toning down Taft's inaugural speech. It isn't clear how bad it was before the Wizard of Tuskegee involved himself, but in the final version Taft said that he wouldn't appoint blacks to office in places where they weren't wanted.[3] This meant none of them would serve in the South at all, or in many places in the North, either.

Shortly after his inauguration Taft made a tour of southern states. Like his Republican predecessors he wanted the Republican Party there to be "lily white." There was no mistaking his position when he went to Charlotte, North Carolina, and gave a speech to the historically black Biddle University, which is now known as Johnson C. Smith University. He told black students that they were "adapted to be farmers," but according to press reports he got applause just the same.[4]

Black Americans were very much disillusioned with the Taft administration, and with good reason. But Taft was followed by Woodrow Wilson, a man who consciously sought to turn back the clock and eliminate any political gains made by black people.

WOODROW WILSON

1913–1921

Woodrow Wilson was born in Virginia in 1856 and also lived in Georgia, North Carolina, and South Carolina as a young man. He vividly remembered meeting Robert E. Lee and watching Union troops occupy his hometown of Staunton, Virginia, in 1865. Ironically, his paternal grandfather was an abolitionist Ohioan, but Wilson's parents had adopted an acceptance of southern culture, including slavery, when they moved south. They were slaveholders and strongly pro-Confederate. They and their son remained unreconstructed throughout their lives.

As president of Princeton University from 1902 to 1910, Wilson made certain that blacks were not allowed to attend. He called their desire for education there "unwarranted." Apparently others at Princeton followed his lead because Princeton didn't have a black graduate until 1946.

After his stint at Princeton, Wilson was elected governor of New Jersey. He ran as the Democratic Party nominee for president in 1912 against Republican incumbent Robert Taft and his predecessor

Theodore Roosevelt, who ran this time on the Bull Moose Party platform. Republican votes were split between Taft and Roosevelt, and Wilson won with 40 percent of the vote. Wilson did not actively campaign for black votes, but in a letter to Bishop Alexander Walters of the African Methodist Episcopal Zion Church he said that he wanted to "assure my colored fellow-citizens of my earnest wish to see justice done them in every matter, and not mere grudging justice, but justice executed with liberality and cordial good feeling. Every guarantee of our law, every principle of our Constitution, commands this, and our sympathies should also make it easy."[1]

Wilson was aided by anger not only at Taft but also at Roosevelt. Lingering bitterness over the handling of the Brownsville soldiers' case created a rift between black Americans and the Republican Party. The letter to Bishop Walters was not the only instance of Wilson saying the right words needed so as to garner black support. Wilson was on his best behavior at a July 1912 meeting with the Equal Rights League. Two years later William Monroe Trotter recalled how he had succumbed: "At that time, we were received open-handed, we Afro-Americans, over the heads of a score of 'non-Afro-Americans,' who were waiting in the anteroom. The governor had us draw our chairs right up around him, and shook hands with great cordiality. When we left he gave me a long handclasp and used such a pleased tone that I was walking on air. What a change between then and now!"[2]

W. E. B. Du Bois and other leaders decided not to side with Roosevelt or Taft but instead supported Wilson. Trotter, a leader of the Niagara Movement, which evolved into the National Association for the Advancement of Colored People (NAACP), supported Wilson in the 1912 election only to watch as the new president lived up to his unreconstructed Confederate upbringing and segregated the federal workforce.

Upon taking office Wilson wasted little time in showing his true colors. Wilson's cabinet members, including Secretary of the

Treasury William McAdoo and Secretary of the Navy Josephus Daniels, played an instrumental role in carrying out governmental Jim Crow segregation. They helped in establishing an apparatus meant to carry out that policy of exclusion. The National Democratic Fair Play Association began to circulate petitions and spread stories of white government employees who didn't want to work with blacks.

Black employees were physically separated from white coworkers; sheets were hung in the middle of offices to separate them. Certain positions were declared completely off-limits for black people. All federal officials, including those under Assistant Secretary of the Navy Franklin D. Roosevelt, were tasked with implementing segregation. Roosevelt personally ordered separate restrooms.[3] Beginning in 1914 all civil service job applicants had to provide photographs — an obvious means of keeping black applicants out. On November 12, 1914, Wilson met again with members of the National Independence Equal Rights League at the White House. This time there was to be no "cordial good feeling." William Monroe Trotter led the delegation with a petition signed by black people in thirty-eight states protesting segregation in federal agencies. The Democratic Party had suffered losses in the recent midterm elections, and Trotter claimed the losses were a reflection of black voters' anger with Wilson. The meeting turned into a shouting match between Trotter and Wilson, which was the only proper outcome. After Trotter mentioned segregation in the postal service and Department of the Treasury, the tense exchange began.

The president said: "If this organization is to have another hearing before me it must have another spokesman. Your manner offends me." I was thunderstruck. I immediately asked in what way I was offensive, and the Chief Executive replied: "Your tone, with its background of passion." I then said, "But I have no passion in me Mr. President, you are entirely mistaken; you misinterpret my earnestness for passion." I then continued my rebuttal and was interrupted by the President, especially when I told him that we could not control the minds of the colored people, and would not if we could on the segregation question. I continued saying: "Two years ago you were regarded as a second Abraham Lincoln," when he stopped me and said he wanted no personal reference. I told him if he would allow me to continue he would see my intent. He said he "was the one to do the interrupting and not me." I then concluded by saying, "Now we colored leaders are denounced in the colored churches as traitors to our race." "What do you mean by traitors?" inquired the President and I replied, "Because we supported the Democratic ticket in 1912."4

A November 13, 1914, *The New York Times* headline summed up the encounter succinctly: "President Resents Negro's Criticism." The major newspaper in New York's black community, *The New York Age*, described the same incident differently: "President of the United States Endorses Segregation as Government Policy." It added for good measure, "Gets Mad with Negroes." If Trotter is remembered for nothing else, he should get credit for this journalistic proof of acting righteously on behalf of black people. The argument was needed, and while Trotter backpedaled upon receiving criticism, he accomplished far more than he would have with politesse.

Author, lawyer, and civil rights pioneer James Weldon Johnson was among those who realized the benefits of the incident: "It is perhaps, after all, a good thing that the incident happened as it did. If Mr. Wilson had listened to the delegation, and made some cautious and perfunctory remarks about 'looking into the matter, etc.,' nobody would ever have known that the Equal Rights committee had waited upon him, and, most probably, nothing would ever have been done."⁵ But Johnson also realized the folly of Trotter, Du Bois, and others who had endorsed Wilson in 1912: "It is incomprehensible where those members of the delegation and other colored men who voted for Wilson two years ago ever got the idea that he would act differently from the way in which he has acted."⁶

If there had been any doubt about where Wilson stood, his promotion of the film *Birth of a Nation* ended it. The film, based on the bestselling novel *The Clansman*, was a paean to white supremacy and a revisionist history of the Reconstruction era. Trotter and others had stopped some stage productions of *The Clansman*, but director D. W. Griffith, a Kentucky-born Confederate defender, nonetheless created the film. The elegiac propaganda piece was performed by white actors in blackface and depicted members of the KKK as heroic figures. Wilson not only liked the film but had a screening in the White House and declared that it was "like writing history with lightning," and "all so terribly true." Trotter, Du Bois, and others attempted to have the movie banned, but the presidential seal of approval won the day. The horrific film is still considered a cinematic classic despite its obvious racist content, and it is used for recruitment purposes by the Ku Klux Klan and other white power hate groups.

But Wilson did more than promote racist film imagery. He did nothing to halt a series of mob attacks against black people in late May and early July 1917 in East St. Louis, Illinois. The death toll from the July massacres in all likelihood exceeded one hundred people. More than six thousand were made homeless. The mob violence in East St. Louis has been attributed to labor competition, with new black migrants from southern states being accused of taking scarce jobs and being used as strikebreakers. The reality was far simpler. One local business leader said, "This is going to be a white man's town hereafter; the blacks will be run out of here and we'll have a white man's town."[7] The Wilson administration did nothing to investigate or to punish the perpetrators, claiming that no federal statutes had been violated.[8] Conversely, black soldiers who fought against a similar attempt at a massacre in Houston, Texas, in August 1917 were convicted of murder, and nineteen of them were executed without being given an opportunity to appeal.

The East St. Louis riots and the punishments inflicted on the black soldiers in Houston generated protest throughout the country. Wilson was again forced to speak to a delegation of black people in 1917. That group was made up of members of the New York branch of the NAACP and was led by James Weldon Johnson. Johnson pleaded with Wilson to make a statement against lynching. But Wilson demurred, claiming that his words would have no "special effect." Wilson was polite and Johnson, who had been a harsh critic, was somewhat mollified: "When I came out, it was with my hostility toward Mr. Wilson greatly shaken; however, I could not rid myself of the conviction that at bottom there was something hypocritical about him."

On July 26, 1918, Wilson did make a statement against mob violence, but he couched his condemnation in terms of the war effort: "We are at this very moment fighting lawless passion. Germany has outlawed herself among the nations because she has disregarded the sacred obligations of law and has made lynchers of her armies. Lynchers emulate her disgraceful example."[9] His effort was tepid, made no reference to the racism that encouraged lynching, and failed even to mention black people by name. But the tradition of wishful thinking among black leadership continued. Johnson praised Wilson's minimal effort: "So it may be that my estimate of Mr. Wilson was actually colored and twisted by prejudice."[10]

While Wilson received a hero's welcome in Paris in 1919 to plan the postwar makeup of the world, black Americans were suffering from even greater violence. The East St. Louis massacres were repeated throughout the country in what became known as the Red Summer. Black people were victims of murder and property destruction in Washington, DC, and in the states of New York, Delaware, Illinois, Virginia, Kentucky, Georgia, Texas, Nebraska, Arizona, Tennessee, Mississippi, Alabama, and, perhaps worst of all in terms of violence committed, Arkansas.

Local newspapers, government officials, and racist groups spread rumors of black soldiers planning murder sprees. Violent reaction to a sharecroppers' strike in Elaine, Arkansas, led to the deaths of more than two hundred people, and the killers included members of active army units. While Wilson wanted to make the rest of the world safe for democracy, he turned a blind eye to terrorism in his own country, terrorism that he had the power to stop.

Wilson is frequently included on lists purporting to prove which presidents were the best. In fact his record as president is one of the worst for black people, an example of white supremacy practiced by the highest office in the land.

— 29 —

WARREN G. HARDING

1921–1923

The trauma of the Wilson administration ended and new hope began after the return of the Republicans, the party of Lincoln, in the 1920 election of Warren G. Harding, governor of Ohio. Harding initially made all of the right noises. He met with James Weldon Johnson several times during the 1920 campaign. The party platform asked Congress "to consider the most effective means to end lynching in this country which continues to be a terrible blot on our American civilization."[1] On April 12, 1921, Harding condemned lynching in a special session of Congress, but he didn't take any of the actions needed to make it become law. On October 26, 1921, Harding attended a fiftieth anniversary celebration of the founding of Birmingham, Alabama. Like every other Republican president who went on a grand southern tour he had a goal of winning over white voters, and he didn't disappoint when he spoke against "social equality," which was the great bugaboo of the day. But he stunned the white half of the integrated audience when he spoke of the patriotism of black soldiers and added, "Let the black man vote when he is fit to vote, prohibit the white man voting when he is unfit to vote." The black audience cheered wildly when Harding added language about "equal educational opportunity."

So desperate were black Americans for affirmation that Harding was praised despite his making it clear that he opposed the dreaded social equality and any amalgamation of the races. Du Bois responded to this never-ending shibboleth of racism: "It is the white race, roaming the world, that has left its trail of bastards and outraged women and then raised holy hands to heaven and deplored 'race mixture.' No, we are not demanding and do not want amalgamation, but the reasons are ours and not yours. It is not because we are unworthy of intermarriage — either physically or mentally or morally . . . we are abundantly satisfied with our own race and blood."[2]

Republican Missouri congressman Leonidas Dyer sponsored the first of many anti-lynching bills in Congress. Dyer's district was in St. Louis, and he was horrified by the mob attacks against his constituents and others in 1917. Republicans were willing to go on record in support of the bill but refused to fight and connived to get southern Democrats to take the blame for the bill's failure, even though their determined inaction was equally at fault. James Weldon Johnson, executive director of the NAACP, wired Harding the day before the Senate vote but was informed of the bill's failure by a White House staffer.

In 1922, W. E. B. Du Bois lamented, "May God write us down as asses if ever again we are found putting our trust in either the Republican or the Democratic Parties."[3] For his part Harding felt unappreciated for his meager efforts. "The Negroes are very hard to please. If they could have half of the Cabinet, seventy-five percent of the Bureau Chiefs, two-thirds of the Diplomatic appointments and all of the Officers to enforce prohibition perhaps there would be a measure of contentment temporarily, but I do not think it would long abide."[4] This statement encapsulates how he and other presidents regarded their black constituents: as a nuisance to be silenced and not citizens worthy of demanding the rights to which they were entitled.

CALVIN COOLIDGE

1923–1929

Harding died after serving just two years in office. The Republican Coolidge administration that succeeded Harding's gave black Americans more lip service and disingenuous efforts to fight racism. The first of many anti-lynching bills died a slow death in the absence of any priority from the president. Coolidge was not the first, nor would he be the last, president to make excuses instead of fighting to protect black people rather than the mobs who killed them at will. To his credit, Leonidas Dyer continued to push his anti-lynching legislation after Harding died, but it failed under Coolidge again in 1923.

Calvin Coolidge served as president during the resurgence of the Ku Klux Klan. Once consigned to the activity of southern mobs, the KKK again became a potent political force across the country in the 1920s. Neither Coolidge nor most other political leaders would openly denounce them. When forty thousand Klan members marched past the White House in August 1925, the president lived up to the nickname *Silent Cal*: He made certain to be away on vacation and issued no statement at all.

Coolidge was a proponent of "lily white" Republicanism and in 1924 supported removing black delegates from the Republican National Convention; ultimately a chicken-wire screen separated black delegates from whites there. But Coolidge was not just a do-nothing president; he harbored all the racist feelings common to white America. Bruce Barton, the advertising executive who gave the president the best public relations in the grand tradition of American marketing, reported these words Coolidge delivered to a black audience: "The Anglo-Saxon race has been centuries in reaching its present position and . . . the Negro could not and must not expect to bridge the chasm in a century."[1]

The alleged superiority of the Anglo-Saxon Coolidge was nowhere to be found in his dealings with black people. Activist and organizer Marcus Garvey was targeted by a young FBI agent named J. Edgar Hoover during the Wilson and Harding administrations. Garvey had little to show for his Back-to-Africa movement. His Black Star steamship line failed, yet none of those who had made donations managed to make any official complaint. Nevertheless Garvey was convicted of mail fraud for misrepresenting the company and began serving a prison term in 1925. Attorney General John Sargent was concerned not about justice for Garvey but about the obvious prosecutorial misconduct. "This is by no means a healthy condition of affairs," Sargent opined, but his solution to keeping Garvey from becoming a martyr to black people was equally unhealthy. He advised the president to commute Garvey's sentence but ordered him deported to his native Jamaica, where he was disappeared and rendered unable to speak out against the injustice of his case.

Coolidge helped to perpetrate one of the worst mass atrocities against black people since the days of slavery. In 1927 the Mississippi River suffered from a thousand-year flood that killed hundreds and left six hundred thousand people homeless. The flooding took place in the Delta regions of Mississippi, Arkansas, and Louisiana, where black residents already toiled under an oppressive share-cropping debt peonage system. They were forced into labor camps and held at gunpoint. The planter class wanted to make sure they could not flee after the floodwaters receded. The black laborers were forced to pay for Red Cross rations, which in some cases were stolen from them. The NAACP complained bitterly to Secretary of Commerce Herbert Hoover, who instead worked with Robert Moton, the successor to Booker T. Washington, to cover up the government's crime. The Commerce Department took no prisoners in denying the charges and attacking all those who brought attention to the case. "[We managed] to call [off] most of the dogs," said a White House aide, "except one Walker [*sic*] White . . . a Negro who looks like [a] white man and has set himself up as a champion of his race . . . Literally the nigger in the wood pile."[2]

Coolidge worked in silence, but he continued to do damage to black people. Perry Howard, one of the few remaining black Republican officeholders in Mississippi, was accused of buying and selling public offices. J. Edgar Hoover gave him special attention, too. But there was no evidence against Howard, and in the end the president settled for driving Howard and three others out of Republican leadership in 1928.

Walter White was prescient about all these events: "Eventually the Republicans will absorb the anti-Negro South and become, through compromises necessary to gain that end, the relatively anti-Negro party, while the Negro will find refuge in the Democratic Party controlled by the North where in ten states the Negro today holds the balance of power."[3] It took four more decades, but White was ultimately proved correct.

HERBERT HOOVER

1929–1933

Herbert Hoover's family were abolitionist Iowa Quakers. When his parents died and left him orphaned at the age of ten he was raised by his uncle, who had run an Underground Railroad station in his hometown. But Hoover's public life gave no indication of his descent from people who believed in racial justice.

Hoover studied geology at Stanford University and worked in mining in Australia and China as a young man. Those travel experiences did not give him an open mind about non-white people. His observations of Australian Aboriginals were blatantly racist. In a letter to a friend he wrote, "They have a devil-devil, who is not a spirit but a real live nigger, who acts as executioner for the tribe and is therefore the medicine man's partner."[1] In his book *Principles of Mining* he continued in that vein, saying that "Asiatics and negroes" were of a "low mental order" and that "one white man equals from two to three of the colored races, even in the simplest forms of mine work such as shoveling."[2]

Bigoted beliefs such as these were acceptable at the time, and they had real-life consequences, especially when held by powerful people. Hoover was secretary of commerce under Calvin Coolidge and was personally responsible for the criminal treatment of black Mississippi Delta residents during the 1927 flood.

Hoover continued the "lily white" policies that were employed in an ultimately futile effort to attract white southerners to the Republican Party. His nomination of North Carolina segregationist John Parker to the Supreme Court was seen as a direct attack on black people. Parker had once said, "The participation of the Negro in politics is a source of evil and danger to both races." Even the accommodationist Robert Moton, whom Hoover had hired to lead the Colored Advisory Commission formed to investigate allegations of abuses following the 1927 flood, opposed the nomination, telling Hoover that he could not support a man who "so openly declared his contempt."

Hoover's response to opposition was particularly vicious. White House aides called upon Congress and FBI director J. Edgar Hoover to investigate the NAACP for possible communist ties when that group led the anti-Parker effort.[3] Hoover was furious when the nomination was defeated in the Senate. He never forgave the defeat and lambasted those Republicans who joined in the no vote, saying that they "ran like white mice" in the face of criticism.

After Hoover lost to Franklin Roosevelt in the 1932 election he suddenly became interested in the fight against lynching. He had said little on the subject when he was president and had the power to stop mob violence. But the lame duck now imagined himself directing "the modern expedition, through aerial and motor forces of Federal troops located at all important centers throughout the country."[4] His imaginary effort was certainly laughable. But his successor wouldn't do any better.

FRANKLIN D. ROOSEVELT

1933–1945

Franklin Delano Roosevelt benefited from comparisons with his predecessors. To say that he was a better president for black people than Herbert Hoover does not mean that he lived up to his reputation as a groundbreaking liberal, however. It's true that he served in office during the Great Depression and World War II. He changed the office of the presidency, and Americans' expectations of it, forever. It is no exaggeration to call him a larger-than-life figure when his portrait adorned so many American homes during his time in office. But America is a country of low political expectations. Franklin Roosevelt has received far more credit for his treatment of black Americans than he is actually due, even though he and his wife, Eleanor Roosevelt, were beloved by black people both during and after his time in office.

The Democratic Party was the party of the segregated South. The politics of that region had changed little since the days of the Civil War. White southerners were almost uniformly Democrats. Black voters had little reason to leave what they felt were the safer confines of the Republican Party in 1932. Roosevelt had served in the segregationist Wilson administration and chose Texan John Nance Garner as his running mate. Northern Democrats like FDR depended on white southerners and happily used the need to appeal to these constituents to excuse their own inaction on civil rights legislation. FDR never supported anti-lynching legislation. It was convenient for him to say that he wanted to help but had his hands tied by the South. Roosevelt banned black reporters from his press conferences from the beginning of his administration and used southern political power as a convenient excuse. He issued a tepid statement that condemned lynching, but only after two white men were murdered by a San Jose, California, mob.

Future Supreme Court justice Thurgood Marshall told a revealing story about Roosevelt's phony concern for black people. Marshall went to Attorney General Francis Biddle to seek his help in the case of a black man accused of murdering a white sheriff in Virginia. Biddle called the president with the intention of discussing the matter and asked Marshall to listen to the conversation on another phone. He was stunned to hear Roosevelt say, "I warned you not to call me again about any of Eleanor's niggers. Call me one more time and you are fired."[1]

Both Roosevelts used black people in photo opportunities to appear as if they were taking black people's concerns seriously. Mary McLeod Bethune, president of historically black Bethune-Cookman College and founder of the National Conference of Negro Women, became one of the go-to people who helped the Roosevelts appear more progressive than they actually were. At a time when black people were ignored and left without legal protections, it is understandable that the sight of Bethune having tea with Mrs. Roosevelt would be a cause for celebration and admiration. Though she did not run for elective office, Eleanor Roosevelt was a politician in her own right, and she used those skills at opportune moments to carry out public relations campaigns. Her decision to resign from the Daughters of the American Revolution in 1939 may have been a decision of principle, but it also showed her political acumen. The DAR barred opera singer Marian Anderson and other black performers from their stage at DAR Constitution Hall. Roosevelt resigned from the organization and arranged for Anderson to sing at the Lincoln Memorial on Easter Sunday in 1939, skillfully making her point without appearing to be too close to Anderson. She didn't attend the concert herself, and she referred to the incident in her syndicated column, "My Day," without mentioning Anderson by name.

The First Lady knew the power of her office, and she knew that dispensing crumbs at the right moment to a desperate and oppressed people would give her more credit than she deserved. She penned a now-famous article in the *Negro Digest* in 1943. In "Freedom: Promise or Fact" she opined that "if I were a Negro today, I think I would have moments of great bitterness." The acknowledgment may seem good until she added, "I think, however, that I would realize that if my ancestors had never left Africa, we would be worse off as 'natives' today."[2]

President Roosevelt used much the same strategy in his dealings with black people. He never made a direct reference to black people or to civil rights legislation. As president during the Depression he brought about basic legislation such as the Social Security Act, which helped all Americans, but even then he acquiesced to the rest of the white people's party, deliberately excluding agriculture and domestic work from Social Security protection. At the time, most black people still lived in southern states and were largely employed as domestic servants and farmworkers. Even in the North, most black women were employed by white households. Black people may have loved FDR for passing the Social Security Act, but most of them couldn't benefit from it until amendments were enacted in 1950 and 1954.

Any gains accrued to black people during the New Deal era came about because of their own political action, not the largesse of the Roosevelt administration. A. Philip Randolph, president of the Brotherhood of Sleeping Car Porters, instigated one such gain when he threatened a march on Washington in 1941 if the administration did not enact civil rights legislation for black defense workers. On June 25, FDR signed Executive Order 8802, which instituted the Fair Employment Practices Committee (FEPC). Randolph's march was scheduled to take place just one week later, and he called it off but did not disband his organization, the March on Washington Movement. His decision was a wise one. In 1943, Executive Order 9346 gave the FEPC a full-time staff and greater enforcement powers. It is safe to assume that this would not have happened had Randolph not continued his challenge to the Roosevelt administration.

The old slavocracy still held sway in the twentieth century. Black persons were counted as full citizens and no longer as only three-fifths of one as they had from the 1787 Constitutional Convention until the Fourteenth Amendment repealed the compromise in 1868, but they still lived by the whims of people who considered them not fully human. Roosevelt may have had a so-called Black Cabinet, but he was never seen publicly with any of these individuals. Photo opportunities with black people fell under the First Lady's purview.

The Black Cabinet, also called the Federal Council of Negro Affairs, gave a semi-official status to blacks working in federal agencies. It was important only to a point. It certainly benefited those individuals fortunate enough to be in it, but it didn't change the Democrats' allegiance to white southerners. Under FDR, black people stayed in the familiar position of having to be happy with crumbs.

Black people benefited from Roosevelt's programs in the same way that whites did. There was no effort to redress grievances that were unique to the group. Franklin Roosevelt was beloved by black people, but only because he was a master at good public relations and because he made the right enemies among his own class. The tendency to love some presidents who did little for them that was substantive was, and is, a constant for black Americans.

HARRY S. TRUMAN

1945–1953

Harry Truman, who became president upon Roosevelt's death in 1945, represents the contradictions that black Americans face when making political choices. He was openly racist and was a member of the KKK in 1920 when he campaigned for a local judgeship in Missouri. Embarrassed by the act later, he claimed that he had done so under duress and once made the bizarre claim that the Klan had threatened to kill him. Yet Truman is fondly remembered by black people of his era as a president who was "good on civil rights."

His home state of Missouri was a border state — one of four slave states, along with Maryland, Delaware, and Kentucky, that differed from the rest of the South only in that they did not join the Confederacy. Missouri may not have had regular forces on the field of battle, but it was the scene of a ferocious Confederate guerrilla campaign led by Jesse and Frank James and others of their ilk. During Truman's childhood, Frank James would show up in his hometown of Independence, Missouri, for reunions with other elderly veterans of the infamous Quantrill's Raiders. In 1901 the local paper, *The Jackson Examiner*, printed this editorial:

> The community at large need not be especially surprised if there is a Negro lynching in Independence. The conditions are favorable at this time. There are a lot of worthless young Negro men in town who do nothing. They do not pretend to work and stand around on the streets and swear and make remarks about ladies and others who may pass by. They crowd into the electric cars and become offensive.[1]

Truman's grandparents were all slaveholders. His mother recalled as a child watching Union soldiers steal and destroy livestock and lamented that the "white man Lee had to surrender to old Grant." Truman used the word *nigger* his entire life. All defenses of his being "a man of his times" are weasel words used to cover up for the country as a whole: if "Give 'em Hell, Harry" Truman was racist, then so, too, were millions of other Americans.

Truman, like his predecessors, was unconcerned about black Americans' political rights unless their condition threatened his own political fortunes. In 1948 every poll showed the president behind his expected Republican rival, John Dewey. He also faced a challenge from Henry Wallace, who had served as Roosevelt's vice president from 1941 to 1945. Wallace was unceremoniously dumped as FDR's vice presidential candidate in the 1944 campaign in favor of Truman so as to appease southern Democrats eager for a border-state man who wouldn't talk about equality as Wallace had.

South Carolina governor Strom Thurmond led thirty-five southerners out of the 1948 Democratic Party convention in protest of a civil rights platform supported by President Harry Truman. When asked why he was walking out when Roosevelt had had the same platform, he replied, "I agree. But Truman really means it."[2] But the evidence shows that Truman's convictions on the matter were born of political pressure and expedience.

Vice President Truman and President Roosevelt met together only once after the 1944 election, leaving an uninformed man in office in April 1945 who also labored under Roosevelt's shadow. He was seen as a one-term caretaker and had little personal popularity. Wallace was always a favorite of the left wing of the Democratic Party, and his decision to run as the Progressive candidate in 1948 put Truman on the defensive.

Among others, Paul Robeson also put Truman on the defensive. On September 23, 1946, Robeson led a delegation from the American Crusade Against Lynching to a White House meeting with Truman. He began by reading the delegation's statement.

> Mr. President, we are here representing fifteen hundred delegates from various parts of the country, attending a conference to inaugurate an American Crusade to End Lynching. We know that you have received delegations concerned with the rising wave of lynching and mob-violence in the United States, but you have thus far refrained from issuing a formal public statement expressing your views on lynching, and recommending a definite legislative and educational program to end the disgrace of mob violence.

Truman interrupted by saying that he was "thinking about it." Another delegate, Mrs. Harper Sibley, pointed out the contradiction of the United States prosecuting Nazi war criminals while protecting race murder at home. Robeson said that black war veterans might "cause a natural emergency that called for federal intervention."

Robeson was serious in his encounter with Truman and wouldn't defer to him. When Truman claimed that the US and Great Britain were the "last refuge of freedom in the world," Robeson differed. "I disagreed. The British Empire is one of the greatest enslavers of human beings." The meeting became so heated that Truman walked out, but Robeson didn't back down.[3] He spoke at the Lincoln Memorial, testified before Congress, and engaged in pitched battles with the press on the issue. Of course, he paid a personal price: The refusal in 1950 to reissue his passport unless he signed a loyalty oath and an affidavit declaring that he was not a member of the Communist Party was a direct result of his outspokenness toward Truman and others. The aftermath of this episode proved that cajoling, settling for black people in prominent positions, fleeing to one party as a bulwark against the other, and the other usual-suspect methods were less effective than acts of direct confrontation.

Facing election in 1948 as an underdog, Truman had to find a way to appeal to an important part of the Roosevelt constituency: black voters in the North. In November 1947 his aide James Rowe wrote "The Politics of 1948," a forty-page memorandum, erroneously attributed to Clark Clifford until 1991,[4] that showed him a path to victory. Rowe was clear that the president would have to cultivate black voters.

> The Republicans know how vulnerable the Democratic Party is insofar as the negro vote is concerned. They have been bending every effort to woo the negroes away from the Administration's fold. In all probability, Republican strategy at the next session will be to offer an FEPC [Fair Employment Practices Committee], an anti-poll tax bill, and an anti-lynching bill. This will be accompanied by a flourish of oratory devoted to the Civil Rights of various groups of our citizens.
>
> The Administration would make a grave error if we permitted the Republicans to get away with this. It would appear to be sound strategy to have the President go as

far as he feels he possibly could go in recommending measures to protect the rights of minority groups. This course of action would obviously cause difficulty with our Southern friends but that is the lesser of two evils.

If it can be said that Truman was at all "good for black people" it is because he didn't want to be nothing more than an unelected caretaker, a soon-to-be-former president, and a footnote in history. If he wanted to win he had to do something to bring black voters into the fold. On October 29, 1947, the Truman administration released the document "To Secure These Rights." It was a blueprint for civil rights legislation that included desegregation of the military and elimination of poll taxes, which were imposed in southern states.

Truman wavered over his civil rights plans, but A. Philip Randolph forced his hand when he again threatened a Democratic president with a march on Washington if his demands for civil rights legislation were not met. Randolph and Truman met in the White House on March 22, 1948. Truman was proposing a peacetime draft, but Randolph told Truman that blacks would "never bear arms again until all forms of bias and discrimination are abolished." Truman didn't appreciate Randolph's candor and said so: "I wish you hadn't made that statement. I don't like it at all."[5] He then left the meeting, but Randolph was undeterred and later picketed the White House.

Truman also felt pressure at the July 1948 Democratic National Convention. Minneapolis mayor Hubert Humphrey and other northerners insisted on keeping the civil rights platform and ultimately won the day. South Carolina senator Strom Thurmond and other southerners then walked out and formed the States' Rights Democratic Party, popularly known as the Dixiecrats. They held their own convention in Birmingham, Alabama, and Thurmond ran as a presidential candidate on the Dixiecrat ticket.

Truman used his executive order authority to establish the FEPC permanently and desegregate the military on July 26, 1948. He had cast his lot with the electoral advantage he needed and with pressure from A. Phillip Randolph. He did not return to the subject again until just four days before Election Day. On October 29, 1948, he made a campaign stop in Harlem at Dorrance Brooks Square on the corner of 135th Street and St. Nicholas Avenue. It was the first visit to that celebrated neighborhood by a sitting president. Although the visit was not announced until one day earlier, a crowd of more than sixty thousand people lined the streets to greet Truman.

Philleo Nash, the president's special assistant on civil rights, was surprised to find the large crowd quiet before Truman began to speak: "Almost everybody in that crowd was praying, either with his head down or actually was kneeling. They were quiet because they were praying, and they were praying for the President, and they were praying for their own civil rights. And they thought it was a religious occasion."[6]

Devotion to the idea of a savior had not abated since the days of Lincoln. The disappointments and outright betrayals had not changed the hope for salvation from some political figure or party. While Truman did not take the actions he could have and should have to end lynching, his appearance in the community known as the capital of black America was enough to cause celebration. His speech was not particularly illuminating, nor was it even truthful: "I created the Civil Rights Committee because racial and religious intolerance began to appear after World War II. They threatened the very freedoms we had fought to save."[7] As someone who went on a self-described "nigger chase" in 1914, Truman was well aware that racism didn't start after 1945.

The iconic erroneous newspaper headline "Dewey Defeats Truman" showed his thin margin of victory. Black votes in Ohio, Illinois, and California were particularly crucial. Strom Thurmond prevailed in Alabama, Louisiana, Mississippi, and South Carolina. But he had made his point, and Democrats would not easily declare their independence from the Dixiecrat brethren. Truman was motivated by the need for black votes, and the candidacy of Henry Wallace made that need even greater. Black people led by Randolph and other leaders should get credit for moving Truman with their demands.

Despite being anointed with the "good for black people" label, Truman returned to the fold as the unreconstructed descendant of slaveholders in his later years. In 1960, when sit-ins swept the segregated South, Truman declared that he wouldn't countenance such behavior in a business he owned, thereby admitting that he would run a segregated business: "If anyone came into my store and tried to stop business I'd throw him out. The Negro should behave himself and show he's a good citizen. Common sense and good will can solve this thing. We've done it in Missouri."[8] Truman didn't back down when the Detroit branch of the NAACP questioned his remarks: "Your telegram regarding the statement which I made about sit downs in the restaurant is correct. I would do just what I said I would." Truman was so confident of the rightness of this position that he added, "This is not personal nor confidential."[9]

He later added that the demonstrations were communist-inspired. He finally stopped discussing the issue when former secretary of state Dean Acheson wrote him a letter imploring him to do so: "Do not say that they are communist inspired. The evidence is all the other way, despite alleged views of J. Edgar Hoover, whom you should trust as much as you would a rattlesnake with a silencer on its rattle."[10] Harlemites praying for Truman in 1948 were all forgotten when the time came to choose sides in the struggle for real change.

DWIGHT D. EISENHOWER

1953–1961

Dwight Eisenhower does not have a reputation as a "good for black people" president. It is just as well, when the designation is generally based on mythmaking and wishful thinking. It is true that he completed the desegregation of the armed forces that Truman began. He also desegregated public facilities and schools within the District of Columbia. In typical fashion, black people effusively praised Eisenhower for carrying out what were small changes in policy. In 1954, Congressman Adam Clayton Powell proclaimed that Eisenhower "has done more to eliminate discrimination and to restore the Negro to the status of first class citizenship than any President since Abraham Lincoln." The hyperbolic statement was born of decades of black fear and of the need to hope that the party in power at any given moment would do no harm. A tiny bit of progress is then inflated, and even open racists can be praised.

Eisenhower was president during the landmark *Brown v. Board of Education* Supreme Court decision, which ended segregation in public education facilities. It was a watershed moment that influenced not only education but also all public institutions. Jim Crow was on the way out. Black people were not going to turn back, but white people were not going to give up easily, either. It meant that the new Civil War had begun in earnest.

The day after the decision was announced on May 17, 1954, Eisenhower gave these tepid words of support: "The Supreme Court has spoken and I am sworn to uphold the constitutional processes in this country; and I will obey." His administration was even less enthusiastic than those words implied. The Eisenhower Justice Department reacted with panic when the court asked for submission of the customary brief in the case. Deputy Attorney General William P. Rogers responded, with something akin to annoyance, "Jesus, do we really have to file a brief? Aren't we better off staying out of it?"

Even the five justices who ruled in Brown's favor were afraid of the political repercussions. The court had procrastinated for two years before taking the case. William O. Douglas's notes from a December 1952 conference show the depth of anxiety about doing what was obviously right both legally and morally. According to Douglas, Justice Hugo Black worried that "there may be violence" if they ruled in favor of Brown. Felix Frankfurter and Robert Jackson saw that possibility "with great alarm and thought that the Court should not decide the question if it was possible to avoid it." Chief Justice Fred Vinson was more concerned with the "serious practical problems" in desegregating southern schools.[1]

Precisely because of these fears, the justices kicked the can down the road and didn't rule on how or when Brown would be implemented. *Brown* II, which determined implementation of the original decision, was under deliberation when the court reconvened in October 1954. The NAACP brief insisted that segregation be ended immediately with a definitive time limit for complete integration of the schools. Eisenhower made a now-hidden change to the brief that is described as having "toned down the Justice Department's rhetoric that might shame the south."[2]

The Supreme Court case and resulting activism led Eisenhower to do what no other president had done: He hired a black person to fill an executive position in his administration. On July 10, 1955, the White House announced, "Everett Frederic Morrow, a Negro, has been named to a top job in President Eisenhower's Executive Office."[3] Morrow had covered the Eisenhower 1952 campaign for CBS. He was one of the few working black journalists at the time. Eisenhower's chief of staff, Sherman Adams, had urged Morrow to leave CBS in preparation for the appointment, but when he resigned there was no position for him. He waited more than two years before he was appointed administrative officer for special projects.

Morrow had been educated at Bowdoin College and Rutgers University Law School, but when he arrived at the White House even secretaries refused to work for him. When he was officially sworn into office more than three years later, Eisenhower didn't attend the ceremony. Morrow wrote in his journal, "The White House is a little embarrassed about me."[4] He was reduced to ceremonial window dressing.

Eisenhower again faced having to intervene in school desegregation in 1957 when nine black students integrated Central High School in Little Rock, Arkansas. The images of National Guard troops escorting the nine children into school have become iconic, but they shouldn't be used to give Eisenhower undue credit. Eisenhower only sent the troops because Governor Orville Faubus, who had promised to admit the black students, then refused to do so. Martin Luther King had called the president "wishy-washy" on the issue of integration but then sent him a congratulatory telegram when federal action admitted the students.[5]

Eisenhower supported the segregationist obstructions that were euphemistically referred to as states' rights on issues such as the Montgomery Bus Boycott. His administration said nothing about the murder of fourteen-year-old Emmett Till or other lynch law

killings, nor anything in support of desegregation efforts at schools
and universities. He didn't want to deal with civil rights issues or
with black people unless he was compelled to do so by circum-
stance. In private Eisenhower condemned the *Brown v. Board of
Education* ruling, telling a friend, "No single event has so disturbed
the domestic scene in many years as did the Supreme Court's decision of 1954."[6] He opposed desegregation of the military and saw
nothing wrong with black and white university students being
separated by "some kind of railing."[7] He told future Supreme Court
justice Earl Warren that white southerners were "not bad people.
All they are concerned about is to see that their sweet little girls
are not required to sit in school alongside some big, overgrown
Negroes."[8]

Eisenhower's one act of common sense is what historians
constantly tout as a moment of greatness, and it has granted him
credit for far more than he deserves. He was clearly a segregationist and was forced to do the little that he accomplished for black
people.

JOHN F. KENNEDY

1961–1963

In the late 1960s and into the 1970s it was common to see, in black households in America, a portrait of John F. Kennedy, Robert Kennedy, and Martin Luther King; the image was almost obligatory. All three men were assassinated and were forever linked as martyrs. King's bona fides as the leader of a struggle for human rights are secure, but the Kennedy brothers profited from an undeserved reputation. John F. Kennedy enjoyed one of the best marketing/propaganda efforts in modern history. He had great speechwriters, the love of the elite classes, an Ivy League education, and a family who had been famous for decades. Then he was shot to death. His team of image-makers and their friends in media had no trouble burnishing his image.

Kennedy was never fully supportive of the civil rights movement. The Democratic Party still depended on southern Dixiecrats for support, and Kennedy's responses to the liberation struggle were tepid at best. The March on Washington took place just three months before his death, but it happened only after its message was co-opted and watered down by his administration, in particular by his brother Robert, who served as attorney general.

John Kennedy began his road to undeserved sainthood before his election as president. When King was arrested in Atlanta just weeks before the 1960 election, the candidate called Coretta King to express his concern. Robert worked behind the scenes to get King and his colleagues out of jail, and the beginning of yet another "good-for-black-people presidency" myth began. The Reverend Martin King, Sr., proclaimed, "As a Baptist I was going to vote against John Kennedy because he was a Catholic, but if he had the courage to wipe the tears from my daughter-in-law's eyes then I have the courage to vote for him, Catholic or not. And I've got a whole suitcase of votes that I'm taking up and putting in the lap of John Kennedy."[1]

As his campaign song "High Hopes (with John Kennedy)" suggested, there were high hopes that Kennedy would take strong measures on civil rights legislation when he came into office. But he did none of the things that had been discussed even among his advisers. He did not desegregate the National Guard or sue southern states to force school integration. He was initially opposed to issuing executive orders prohibiting discrimination because southerners chaired the House and Senate committees that would have the opportunity to weaken or overturn them.[2]

The first of the executive orders that he ultimately decided to issue, signed on March 6, 1961, required federal contractors to take "affirmative action" against discrimination based on race or color. It was the first official use of the term. The order also established the President's Committee on Equal Employment Opportunity, the forerunner to the establishment of a full-fledged federal agency, the EEOC. The order was toothless, as the president stated at the committee's first meeting that compliance should be voluntary. Cancellation of contracts would be a last resort. One week after the committee was established the defense department awarded a one-billion-dollar contract to the Lockheed Corporation in Marietta, Georgia, which ran a segregated plant and did so on government land.[3]

Another executive order, issued on November 20, 1962, prohibited housing discrimination, but only for newly constructed properties and federally funded projects. The signing of the order was timed to take place after congressional elections so as to maintain the support of southern Democrats.

When activists defied the American apartheid system with freedom rides and demonstrations, the Kennedys were anxious to keep them under control. They asked for a "cooling off" period without these actions in exchange for funding for the Voter Education Project, which informed and encouraged voter registration in the South. Robert Kennedy's rationale for support was cynical: "If enough Negroes registered, they could obtain redress of their grievances internally, without the federal government being involved in it at all."[4] The Southern Christian Leadership Conference (SCLC) took the funding offered, but youth in the Student Nonviolent Coordinating Committee (SNCC) were unhappy and felt that older leaders had been bought off by the Kennedys. SNCC students felt no obligation to live up to any entreaties to "cool off."

While the Kennedy administration asked activists to stand down, it never gave up its effort to make southern segregationists happy. A 1961 omnibus judgeship bill created 130 vacancies, many of which were filled by appointees handpicked by southern senators. The Justice Department even lobbied the American Bar Association to revise a negative assessment of one of the nominees to make him more acceptable during the confirmation process. Both Alabama senators supported the unqualified man, and the administration followed their lead.

Even his televised speech calling civil rights a "moral issue" took place because of the defiance of black people who didn't care about what the Kennedy brothers wanted. George Wallace stood in the doorway of the University of Alabama in an attempt to bar two black students from attending, but it was their determination to attend class that set off the necessary crisis. Kennedy's speech made clear that he was more interested in stopping protest: "We have a right to expect that the Negro community will be responsible and uphold the law, but they have the right to expect the law to be fair."[5]

While Kennedy would hold a photo opportunity with Myrlie Evers, the widow of Medgar Evers, he did nothing to keep people like Evers from being killed by Klansmen in the first place. Despite pleas from Dr. King and others, the administration repeatedly refused to provide protection for people who only wanted to exercise their citizenship rights.

Like the Franklin Roosevelt administration, Kennedy tried to stop the March on Washington. The march was originally called the Poor People's March, and its demands were not limited to passing civil rights legislation but extended to ending poverty in America. The president told the black protesters that their activism was a hindrance to progress rather than its impetus: "We want success in Congress, not just a big show at the Capitol. Some of these people are looking for an excuse to be against us."[6] Robert Kennedy expressed criticism from the very beginning, accusing King of wanting to embarrass his brother. On the eve of the march he spoke to diplomat Marietta Tree, saying about Bayard Rustin's involvement, "So you're down here for that old black fairy's anti-Kennedy demonstration?" When Tree attempted to change the subject to Martin Luther King, Kennedy interjected, "He's not a serious person. If the country knew what we know about King's goings-on, he'd be finished."[7]

The administration was prepared to pull the plug if any of the speeches were deemed too radical for their tastes. The march was considered successful, but for the wrong reasons: "[Kennedy] was pleased that no disruptive incidents had marred an event that had begun as a protest but had ended as a celebration and public relations bonanza for both the movement and for Kennedy's civil rights program."[8]

The assassinations of the Kennedy brothers ensured they would be remembered with more exaltation than either of them deserved. They were always behind, always pushed ahead by the people who insisted on making change. The affection they still inspire is part of a long and sad tradition of black people being pleased with the smallest political victories.

1964–1989

LATE TWENTIETH CENTURY

1965: The Voting Rights Act allows the federal government to oversee election processes in states where rights are restricted.

1966: Huey P. Newton and Bobby Seale found the Black Panther Party for Self-Defense, with its focus on education, voting, safety, and full employment.

1969: Nixon's Office of Minority Business Enterprise supports and assists black-owned businesses.

1973: A federal judge creates one of the first mandated racial quotas for the Bridgeport, Connecticut, Police Department.

1980: There are almost twenty-seven million black people living in the United States.

1980: Black men earn fifty-six cents for every dollar earned by a white man.

1986: After significant pressure from the black public, Congress overrides President Reagan's veto of the Anti-Apartheid Act divesting from South Africa.

LYNDON B. JOHNSON

1963–1969

Lyndon Johnson's racism was well known but is overlooked in the interest of creating a happy narrative. He is remembered as the president who shepherded the Civil Rights and Voting Rights Acts through Congress. When announcing the passage of the Civil Rights Act he famously said, "We shall overcome." He is seen as a champion of the civil rights movement and is considered a president who was "good for black people."

But Johnson did only as much as he was forced to do by the demands of black America. The civil rights movement was a time of intense and dangerous struggle. The tendency to minimize the ordeal and the victory of black liberation must be rejected. The protest was most effective when unfettered by political party allegiance. The people who pushed the politicians, alongside conservatives in the civil rights establishment, created a very necessary crisis and thereby forced Johnson to do what he otherwise would not have. He was, after all, the man who also casually wrote the words "this nigger drives for me"[1] in a letter of permission he gave to his black driver.

One of the people most responsible for making Johnson look good was Fannie Lou Hamer. A Mississippian and lifelong share-cropper, she became a leader in the struggle in that state. She and others formed the Mississippi Freedom Democratic Party (MFDP) in 1964 and selected an integrated slate of delegates for that year's Democratic National Convention in Atlantic City, New Jersey. Johnson was running to be elected president in his own right after ascending to the position when Kennedy was assassinated and, like all Democrats, worried about keeping the segregationist South in the Democratic Party.

The regular Democratic delegates were all white in a state where black people took their lives into their hands if they attempted to vote. Yet the integrated sixty-eight-person MFDP was turned away by the Democratic Party. Initially they were told they would have no vote and would be mere observers. When they flatly rejected that offer the MFDP were told that two members could be "at-large" delegates while the rest would be considered guests. Johnson, Hubert Humphrey, Walter Mondale, Martin Luther King, Whitney Young, and other organizational leaders all argued for the MFDP to accept the compromise.[2] Some within the MFDP wanted to accept the Democrats' offer, but Hamer and others recommended standing fast.

The Johnson administration worked mightily to keep the MFDP from being seated. The FBI had the MFDP under electronic surveillance, as well as King's and Bayard Rustin's telephones. White House special assistant Bill Moyers received the informa-tion, and he and others in the Johnson administration worked hard to prevent the convention credentials committee from seating the MFDP as the legitimate representatives of Mississippi voters.[3]

While the MFDP ultimately refused the compromise and returned to Mississippi empty-handed, Fannie Lou Hamer forced the Democrats to sit up and take notice. She spoke about her ordeal in Winona, Mississippi, after she and others had attempted to register. She was beaten first by black prisoners who were forced to do the dirty work. She was then beaten by a white policeman. As the cameras rolled, a very rattled Lyndon Johnson hastily called a press conference. The media thought he would announce his choice for vice president, but his only goal was to keep Hamer off America's television screens. When he ended saying only that he was commemorating the nine-month anniversary of John F. Kennedy's assassination and the shooting of Texas governor John Connally, some of the networks returned to the convention. Others rebroadcast Hamer's speech later that evening. If anyone should be credited with the passage of the Voting Rights Act in 1965, it is Fannie Lou Hamer and the others who forced federal action.

The actions and the inactions of his predecessors all came to a head for Johnson. Sustained agitation from the liberation movement had brought the Civil Rights Act, Voting Rights Act, and Fair Housing Act into being. But a hundred years of frustration and anger didn't dissipate. After the Voting Rights Act was signed in 1965, the Watts section of Los Angeles exploded into the first of a series of urban uprisings that spread across the country over the next three years.

The tensions created by the escalating Vietnam War and the living conditions of millions of people finally exploded. Johnson was angry and resentful that he was so unappreciated. But there were more surprises awaiting the president. Martin Luther King was himself impacted by the growing anti-war movement. The passage of important legislation had given him an opportunity to see beyond the need to end legal segregation. The people of Watts lived as residents of a colony, without access to basic services, in substandard schools and housing and with the threat of police violence.

When Martin Luther King publicly declared his opposition to the Vietnam War on April 4, 1967, he also broke with Johnson. White America didn't understand. They may have been sympathetic to the Nobel Peace Prize winner and to people attacked with police dogs, but they were dismayed by the Black Panther Party and calls for justice that never seemed to end. Johnson appointed the Kerner Commission to investigate the causes of the urban uprisings, but he wasn't satisfied with the conclusion that the nation comprised two societies, "one black, one white — separate and unequal."

The backlash had begun, and Johnson became a victim. He chose not to run for reelection early in 1968 after watching the urban unrest and continued opposition to the war in Vietnam. American politics had changed, and racist appeals were once again acceptable.

RICHARD M. NIXON

1969–1974

Nixon's victory in 1968 was a reaction against the liberation movement of the 1960s. A return to "law and order" was his campaign theme, a not-subtle attack on the activism of the previous decade, and in particular a dog whistle to white racists rattled by the anger that erupted into violence following the murder of Martin Luther King.

Nixon won a three-way race against Democratic vice president Hubert Humphrey and Alabama governor George Wallace, a segregationist Democrat who ran as an independent. The combination of total votes for Nixon and Wallace proved that white America wanted to be finished with black people and their demands for citizenship rights. Nixon did not disappoint and began the process of openly using racism to gain political support. Ironically, he also enacted policies that were helpful to many black people.

There was great gloom in black America in 1968. Lyndon Johnson was still seen as a savior after his legendary arm-twisting brought the Civil Rights and Voting Rights Acts into being. But the Vietnam War upended his tenure, and when Senator Eugene McCarthy proved to be a viable opponent for the Democratic nomination Johnson withdrew his reelection bid. That political tumult was followed by the assassination of Martin Luther King on April 4, 1968, and of Robert Kennedy on June 5, 1968.

Nixon made overt appeals to white racism with his campaign to bring back "law and order." He actively opposed school busing as a tool of integration and made clear his intent to turn back the clock to the days when white people were not forced to be discomfited by black people's demands. His administration began with orders to slow down school desegregation plans, a first since the *Brown* decision in 1954. He nominated two southern segregationists as Supreme Court justices, although both were rejected by the Senate.

To black people, it looked like the end of the changes they had worked for so relentlessly. The presidential election results showed a clear reaction against them and their demands for citizenship rights. Nixon's election seemed like the end of their political world, augmented by his having advisers like the controversial Daniel Moynihan, who urged "benign neglect" of the troublesome black masses.

Yet it was Nixon who established the Office of Minority Business Enterprise (OMBE), which helped black businesses acquire government contracts. The terms *quota* and *set-asides* are now radioactive to politicians, but it is Nixon who brought them into reality with the OMBE.

Nixon left a contradictory legacy. In 1973 he outlined a health care plan that looked much like Barack Obama's later Affordable Care Act, which perhaps ought to have been given the moniker *Nixoncare* instead of *Obamacare*. As twenty-first-century Republicans made repeal of the ACA a centerpiece of their initiatives, it should be remembered that only forty years earlier, conservative think tanks like the Heritage Foundation recommended a similar health care plan.

But one of Nixon's worst and most enduring legacies was the return to normalized racism. Vice President Spiro Agnew was his attack dog and became known as "Nixon's Nixon." Agnew bragged, "Dividing the American people has been my main contribution to the national political scene. I not only plead guilty to this charge, but I am somewhat flattered by it."[1] Strategist Kevin Philips honed the message of Democratic Party identification with black people and made clear what success would look like: "White Democrats will desert their party in droves."

Nixon's attacks on the civil rights movement were not just rhetorical. During his tenure FBI director J. Edgar Hoover instituted the Counter Intelligence Program (COINTELPRO), the purpose of which was to "expose, disrupt, misdirect, discredit, or otherwise neutralize the activities of black nationalist, hate-type organizations and groupings, their leadership, spokesmen, membership, and supporters." The number of "ghetto-type informants" more than doubled, from thirty-three hundred under Johnson to seventy-five hundred under Nixon. The Nixon administration considered a campaign against Coretta Scott King and sought to undermine Ralph Abernathy's influence as successor at the Southern Christian Leadership Conference.[2]

In the meantime the two major political parties had switched their bases of support. The civil rights movement had completely changed the political allegiance of black voters. White southerners began trending away from the Democrats, and the South became the heart of the Republican Party. Code words and dog whistles changed the face of politics in the United States. Republican strategist Lee Atwater said, "By 1968 you can't say 'nigger' . . . So you say things like forced busing, states' rights."[3]

This strategy of thinly veiled racial divisiveness found great success. Except for Jimmy Carter's one term from 1977 to 1981, Republicans won every presidential contest from 1968 until 1992. The Democrats also took notice and became more conservative and more anti-black in response to Republican success. But if anyone could have predicted that a future Democratic president, the first black president, would claim a right to kill without charge or trial, or that another Democrat would create a mass incarceration state for black people, Nixon might not have fared so badly in comparison.

GERALD R. FORD

1974–1977

Gerald Ford was an accidental president. He became Nixon's vice president in 1973 when Vice President Spiro Agnew resigned after a felony conviction. Nixon himself resigned in August 1974 as he was on the verge of being impeached for his role in the Watergate scandal. Ford was the only president in American history who was not elected to the position of president or vice president.

Ford came to office after many civil rights battles had been fought. The Voting Rights and Civil Rights Acts had become law. He presided over a new chapter in history as de jure school desegregation and affirmative action became the battlegrounds of America's never-ending fight against its racist founding. Ford had been a northern Republican congressman during the time when segregation was the bastion of white southern Democrats. Like other Republicans he voted in favor of the landmark civil rights legislation, but he became president after Nixon had successfully reversed the political polarity and made the Republicans the white party.

Forced busing was the term used to appeal to white America in the 1970s. Like *states' rights*, *quotas*, and the *war on drugs*, it was a means of communicating opposition to black civil and citizenship rights. The April 20, 1971, unanimous Supreme Court ruling in *Swann v. Charlotte-Mecklenburg County* paved the way for busing children into otherwise segregated public schools to achieve the desegregation ordered by the 1954 *Brown* decision. The Swann case ignited a firestorm of protest, violence, and ultimately the wholesale departure of white families from public school systems around the country.

Barely two weeks into his administration, Ford made clear that he was sticking with Republican Party strategy on this issue: "I am opposed to the forced busing of school children because it does not lead to better education and it infringes upon traditional freedoms in America."[1] Thanks to Nixon's southern strategy, white America now had a friend in the Republican Party. Opposition to school desegregation plans was the means of achieving solid support for the Republicans as the new party of and for white America.

On May 27, 1976, Ford said that his Justice Department would look to review the *Brown* decision, which had long been accepted as the law of the land. His press secretary backpedaled the very next day, saying that the president had made an "incorrect reference" to the *Brown* case and had meant to point out subsequent decisions related specifically to busing. The words may have been an inelegant gaffe, but they were uttered because Ford knew that not-so-subtle racism won the day politically.

Boston, Massachusetts, became the epicenter of the busing fight when a federal judge ordered a school busing plan in October 1974. Like Eisenhower, Ford straddled the fence, saying that he disagreed with the court order but expected Boston to "respect the law." The reaction from white neighborhoods in Boston was violent. Black people were attacked in the streets and even pro-busing Senator Edward Kennedy had to flee from a mob attempting to overturn his car. Both the mayor of Boston and the governor of Massachusetts requested National Guard troops, but Ford refused to provide them. Ultimately the administration did not challenge the Boston court order, but Ford continued his appeals to white American racism.

On June 5, 1976, Ford made clear his belief that segregation of private schools was acceptable when he was asked if he would approve of a private school turning someone away on the basis of color. His reply was a classic tactic from the racist playbook: "Individuals have rights. I would hope they would not, but individuals have a right, where they are willing to make the choice themselves, and there are no taxpayer funds involved."[2] Ford had contradicted his own Justice Department, and his interpretation that private schools could discriminate against black children would be overruled by a Supreme Court decision just a few weeks later.

Gerald Ford was a classic American president. He played to the racial demands of white people and hoped not to be called on his chicanery. But fate called him out. His status as an unelected president, his pardon of Nixon, and an economic downturn all undid him. He was succeeded by a southern Democrat who managed to get black votes while also evoking the same racist tropes as his Republican predecessors.

JIMMY CARTER

1977–1981

Jimmy Carter won the presidency in 1976 with more than 90 percent of the black vote. This overwhelming degree of support came about despite the fact that Carter made blatant appeals to white racism during the presidential primaries, including his statement that "I see nothing wrong with ethnic purity being maintained. I would not force racial integration of a neighborhood by government action."[1] Carter proved that the Democrats, having now become the black people's party, could count on that support regardless of what they said or did. Carter ran as a candidate of the "new South," meaning that he wasn't an overt racist like George Wallace and his ilk. He could not have become the governor of Georgia without black voter support, but he was far more conservative than those constituents. Even a cursory examination of his campaign statements indicated that he was no friend of policies that black voters favored. Carter was in fact a strong advocate of neo-liberalism and opposed the traditional black political agenda.

Carter had a typical childhood for a white rural Georgian. He hunted and fished with black playmates, but they attended segregated schools and churches. He was cared for by black women who were paid only one dollar per week for their services. That background was not conducive to thinking of black people as equals who had rights that ought to be respected.[2]

The black political agenda was clear, but Carter felt no need to advocate for the people he needed in order to win. Full employment legislation is an example of how the conundrum played out in the 1976 campaign. The Congressional Black Caucus first proposed full employment legislation in 1971. The Humphrey-Hawkins Full Employment Act was proposed in 1977. Cosponsored by caucus member Augustus Hawkins and Minnesota senator Hubert Humphrey, the bill was originally envisioned as an effort to force the federal government to use its spending authority to create jobs. Carter ignored this centerpiece of black politics until he ran into trouble with his statements about ethnic purity, including that "the government ought not to take as a major purpose the intrusion of alien groups into a neighborhood simply to establish their intrusion."[3]

The uproar over "black intrusion" and "alien groups" forced Carter, then governor of Georgia, to give something to his critics. After enduring days of uproar once the "ethnic purity" statement was dug up from the sixteenth paragraph of a *New York Daily News* interview, he gave mild support to Humphrey-Hawkins. Once in office he did little to help the legislation, which was finally passed and signed into law by Carter in 1978. By that time it was identified as "race-specific." Carter used the fear of inflation to put it on the legislative back burner. Amendments made the act largely symbolic. It would not go into effect unless the rate of inflation was 3 percent in 1983 and 0 percent in 1988. The end result was a bill that would never be acted upon.[4]

Despite an endorsement from Martin Luther King, Sr., when the "ethnic purity" remark damaged his 1976 presidential prospects, in 1979 Carter declared himself neutral on making Martin Luther King's birthday a national holiday. The vote lost to a measure that would have made it a Sunday celebration and hence not a paid federal holiday. It fell to Carter's successor, Ronald Reagan, to make King's birthday a federal holiday.

The Republicans' southern strategy was thrown off-course temporarily because Jimmy Carter was a white southerner. The transformation of the white South from Democrat to Republican was not yet complete, and the prospect of seeing one of their own in the office directed enough white southern voters to Carter to temporarily interrupt the Republican effort. Ultimately the Iranian hostage crisis and a lackluster debate performance against Ronald Reagan sealed Carter's fate in his reelection campaign. His administration was yet another low point for black people, who had again rallied around someone who did little for them. Carter appointed more black people to the federal judiciary and kept some minority set-aside programs to ensure that the government continued to employ black people, but overall the level of support he received was not commensurate with good outcomes for black people. He was succeeded by a man who truly had a mandate to turn back the clock and who continued the long decline of black political life in the modern era.

RONALD REAGAN

1981–1989

Ronald Reagan conducted his 1980 presidential campaign with unconcealed racist sentiments. This political strategy was not a new one for him. He had been making overt appeals to white racism ever since his first days as a politician in California, where he ran for governor in 1966. Reagan denounced the Civil Rights Act of 1964 and the 1965 Voting Rights Act as "humiliating to the south." During his gubernatorial campaign he was in favor of Proposition 14, which made housing discrimination legal. He said that the proposition was important in "upholding the right of a man to dispose of his property or not dispose of it as he sees fit."[1] Even though two years later he criticized the proposition as "not a good measure," his previous words show the degree to which he pandered to racist voters.

It seemed odd at first for Reagan's presidential campaign kickoff to take place in Mississippi. His home state was Illinois, and he was governor of California. Why Philadelphia, Mississippi? The rationale was obvious and cynical. Philadelphia was infamous as the location where three men — James Chaney, Michael Schwerner, and Andrew Goodman — were killed during the Freedom Summer, a 1964 effort to register black voters. Reagan didn't choose the location by throwing darts at a map. He not only went to a place famous for its role in the white supremacist terror that struck at the heart of the liberation movement, but he also spoke there of his support for "states' rights," the moniker of reaction and racist defiance. Those words were the clarion call of the Dixiecrats and the dead-ender segregationists who fought against the tide of a new movement.

Reagan's words in Mississippi were followed by more unconcealed appeals to white grievance. He told the story of a woman dubbed the "welfare queen" by the *Chicago Tribune*. She was a con artist who used various aliases to fraudulently collect eight thousand dollars in benefits. The amount grew with each telling, and she soon was accused of stealing more than $150,000. Reagan also recounted the story of a "strapping young buck" who used food stamps to buy T-bone steaks and other gourmet foods. He may as well have said the fictitious man was black: *Buck* is an anachronistic but colorful word with the same connotation.

Reagan worked the southern strategy better than Nixon or Carter could ever have dreamed of doing. He began an attack on affirmative action programs, turning the civil rights division into a tool for ending set-asides and other remedies for discriminatory outcomes. The goal of his domestic policy was to appease the people who became known as Reagan Democrats — white working-class voters who crossed their traditional party lines to vote for Reagan. As one study indicated, they were united by distaste for blacks: "Blacks constitute the explanation for their vulnerability and for almost everything that has gone wrong in their lives; not being black is what constitutes being middle class; not living with blacks is what makes a neighborhood a decent place to live."[2]

Every aspect of the federal government was used to turn back the clock to the days when segregation was perfectly legal. Reagan appointed William Rehnquist as chief justice of the Supreme Court. As a SCOTUS clerk in 1953, Rehnquist had opined that "*Plessy* was right and should be affirmed."[3] The administration continued to go the extra mile in making points for white racism.

Reagan created a new political language, appropriating the words of his adversaries and turning their ideas against them. Reaganites would quote Martin Luther King as they made plans to reduce or end civil rights regulations. They claimed to want a color-blind society. They didn't want the legal enforcement that would bring this about, so they obscured the conversation with confusion. They used the word *revolution*, a Reagan revolution to describe a wholesale change in how government had worked since the days of Franklin Roosevelt's New Deal. A conservative movement emerged that claimed to care for those at the bottom and referred to the help they needed as a harmful dependency.

Reagan's racist political playbook led him to victory in two landslide elections. In 1988 his vice president, George H. W. Bush, followed the playbook even more closely. Bush went on to victory and continued the tradition of racist infamy that his former boss had maintained. Black Americans watched as the gains they had made in the 1960s eroded one by one. The political trajectory of the country had changed for good, and even future Democratic presidents sounded more like Reagan than like Lyndon Johnson.

1990–2019

MODERN DAY

1990: The black population in the United States is close to forty million.

2008: More than 65 percent of eligible black voters turn out in the election that produces the first black president of the United States.

2013: Trayvon Martin's murder sparks the formation of the Black Lives Matter movement.

2015: Black men still earn less than 75 percent of white men's hourly earnings.

2016: Donald Trump's election revives the openly racist political campaign.

41

GEORGE H. W. BUSH

1989–1993

George Herbert Walker Bush was the product of a Republican family, though in comparison with those of more recent politicians their views might now be seen as more liberal than they were at the time. His father, Connecticut senator Prescott Bush, chaired his state's United Negro College Fund. When the younger Bush moved to Texas and went into the oil business he initially stuck with the northern version of the Republican Party. In 1963 he told a reporter that he "did not think the Republican Party should be a rallying place for segregationists." He established an organization of black Republicans called the Republican Alliance. But Bush saw what had to be done to win a statewide election in Texas, and comity went out the window when he ran for a Senate seat in 1963 by supporting states' rights. He called the 1964 Civil Rights Act "trampling on the Constitution" and warned that it would "displace" white workers.

When Bush ran for the Republican presidential nomination in 1988 he went full tilt to the darker side of his party and its southern, Reagan Democrat strategy. Reagan's use of the welfare queen to elicit white voter support was child's play compared to the Bush campaign's use of a black criminal as a campaign surrogate in 1988. William J. Horton, Jr., was convicted of murder in Massachusetts in 1974 and was eligible for a prison furlough program. He was released on nine occasions without incident, but in 1987 he fled to Virginia, where he assaulted a man and raped his fiancée. This news story was gold to campaign manager Lee Atwater, a South Carolinian and protégé of former Dixiecrat presidential candidate Strom Thurmond. Many states had prison furlough programs, including California, and furloughed prisoners had committed two murders during Ronald Reagan's term as governor. Reagan apologized, yet he allowed the program to continue. But Reagan wasn't running for president in 1988, and neither he nor any Republican suffered from the dreaded "Negro-Democratic mutual identification." The term was coined by Kevin Phillips, a Reagan campaign aide. The expression may be long and wordy, but the point is simple: If Democrats were identified as the black people's party, "white Democrats will desert their party in droves."[1]

Having successfully used William Horton, who was never known by the name *Willie* except by the Bush administration to perpetuate racial stereotypes, to get elected, Bush named Atwater as chairman of the Republican National Committee. There Atwater continued his efforts to ensure white support by demonizing black people and anything connected with them. The Bush administration used the word *quotas* to stigmatize programs guaranteeing black participation in government. It was a signal to his followers, telling them to oppose or support legislation and policy. If black people and Democrats supported anything, Bush was against it.

Senator Edward Kennedy pushed a civil rights bill that would strengthen anti-discrimination laws that had been weakened by a 1989 Supreme Court case. Bush ultimately signed the Civil Rights Act of 1991 after a veto of a previous version, which he dubbed a "quota bill." That year he also nominated Clarence Thomas to succeed the retiring Thurgood Marshall on the Supreme Court. Thomas was as conservative as Marshall was liberal and as chair of the Equal Employment Opportunity Commission had worked hard to oppose everything that agency was meant to do. He rejected all class action lawsuits and went down the line with the administration in claiming that every civil rights remedy was laden with the dreaded "quotas."

The Thomas nomination was a political masterstroke. The civil rights leadership was flummoxed, not knowing how to respond to a black man whose politics would have garnered their opposition had he been white. The politics of the Thomas nomination made for strange bedfellows. *Baltimore Sun* reporter Arch Parsons, a personal friend of Thomas, made entreaties to NAACP president Benjamin Hooks to support Thomas and told White House staff about the conversations.[2] When this intervention by a White House reporter — whose journalist ethics required neutrality — became known, Parsons defended his actions by saying, "I felt there needed to be a black replacement for Thurgood Marshall on the bench. It was important enough for me to overlook my ethical responsibilities." In other words, for Bush, Parsons, and many others, Thomas's skin color trumped his record on issues that deeply affected the lives of black Americans.

Bush's relationship with black America was always informed by cynicism. He used William Horton and the fear of quotas to get elected. He used a little-known judicial nominee to get a conservative court appointment and one whose race silenced those who would otherwise have opposed him. Yet Bush is also known for an action that no other president had taken up until that time: He used the powers of the federal government to prosecute racist police brutality. America was riveted in 1991 by a video showing a Los Angeles black man named Rodney King being beaten by police. The 1992 acquittal sparked riots in which fifty-four people lost their lives. The Bush Justice Department then began prosecution of the police, who were convicted in 1993 during the Clinton administration. Ultimately, two served time in jail.

George H. W. Bush can be given credit for at least one deed that brought justice to the perpetrators of a great injustice. But throughout his tenure he proved that anti-black racism was so potent that future presidential campaigns would use the same strategy to boost their chances of success.

BILL CLINTON

1993–2001

In 1998, Nobel Prize–winning novelist Toni Morrison said of Bill Clinton that "white skin notwithstanding, this is our first black President. Blacker than any actual black person who could ever be elected in our children's lifetime."[1] Morrison was no more prescient than anyone else and had no idea that ten years later there would, in fact, be a black president of the United States. The comment is memorable today for another reason.

By 1998, in the middle of his second term, Bill Clinton had made it clear that black people could be used to get votes but would be betrayed whenever they became a political liability. Once again the ruse of the two-party system, with the designation of one as the white people's party, created massive cognitive dissonance among black people. In some cases, Clinton did the disparaging himself, finding new ways to use black individuals or the entire group as the object of all hate, fear, and anger in the minds of white people.

Black Americans originally had great affection for Bill Clinton for the simple reason that he was a Democrat. Neither he nor any other presidential contender was worthy of great adulation, but the desperation over huge Democratic losses in the last three presidential elections gave Clinton an enormous amount of goodwill. He was also a masterful politician who used the media to great effect. He appeared on *The Arsenio Hall Show* playing a saxophone and wearing dark glasses, a savvy decision in an era when image-making can be as important as policy pronouncements. His ability to show some degree of cool didn't hurt him any and was the beginning of the "first black president" designation.

Even though Clinton appeared on a popular television show with a black host whose audience was known for its hipness, the tried-and-true methods of racial demonization remained part of the path to the White House. Clinton showed his disdain for the black voters he depended on when he left the thick of the campaign trail to oversee the execution of a black man in Arkansas. Ricky Ray Rector had attempted suicide after shooting two men to death in 1981. He had survived the bullet wound to his head, but he had in effect lobotomized himself. He was not competent to stand trial or to assist in his defense. His appeal went all the way to the Supreme Court in 1991, but the court declined to hear it. Rector was so impaired that he thought he would return to his cell and finish his last meal, and so he asked if his dessert could be saved "for later" — in other words, after his execution.

All black Americans were victims of the Clinton 1992 campaign. For the first time in thirty years the Democratic Party platform did not contain any reference to redress of racial injustice.[2] Clinton and his running mate, Al Gore, published a campaign manifesto titled *Putting People First*, which mentioned civil rights only to decry the use of quotas to fight discriminatory practices.[3] These sins of omission were not even the worst racist acts committed by the Bill Clinton campaign.

On March 1, 1992, Bill Clinton held a photo opportunity at Stone Mountain, Georgia.[4] The mountain in the name has the biggest bas-relief sculpture in the world, which depicts Robert E. Lee, Stonewall Jackson, and Jefferson Davis. In 1915 the first of many Ku Klux Klan rallies was held at the site featuring the now-iconic burning crosses.

Clinton had already executed Ricky Ray Rector, so there should have been no need to burnish his crime-fighting credentials. But the Super Tuesday primary was one week away. There were still a few white southern conservatives in the Democratic Party, and Super Tuesday was created to give them a greater voice in the nominating process. They were not to be disappointed when Clinton posed with inmates from the Stone Mountain Correctional Facility as a human backdrop. Nearly all of the men in prison uniforms were black, and Clinton used them to declare that toughness on crime and the evoking of segregationist memory were not unique to Republicans.

But there was more race-baiting to come. On June 13, 1992, Clinton used remarks made by rap singer Sister Souljah to embarrass the Reverend Jesse Jackson, himself a candidate for the Democratic nomination for president in the previous two elections, while at a Rainbow Coalition event. After the police who were videotaped beating Rodney King were acquitted in Los Angeles, riots broke out in the city's South Central neighborhood. Sister Souljah was quoted as saying, "If black people kill black people every day, why not have a week and kill white people?" Her argument was that if society accepted the murder of black people by other black people, the murder of white people should not be regarded any differently. Clinton did more than repudiate her words: With Jesse Jackson looking on, he also compared her to Klansman David Duke. More than twenty years later, the term *Sister Souljah moment* is still part of the political lexicon, used to indicate a politician's rejection of supposedly extreme perspectives and cynical dismissal of supporters for electoral gain.

Even worse than Clinton's personal betrayal of Jackson was the reaction of black "leaders" to the rhetorical ambush. They were either nonchalant or so desperate for victory that they supported the anti-black race-baiting. Congressman John Lewis gave a typical response: "I think what we are witnessing is what I call a quiet revolution in American politics. In the communities I deal with, people want to win, they want to see a Democrat in the White House . . . They understand that in order to win, it is necessary to bring back those individuals who had left the party."[5] His term *individuals who had left the party* obviously meant white people.

When Clinton was inaugurated in 1993 he stuck with what had been a winning formula. In May of that year he nominated Lani Guinier to head the Department of Justice Civil Rights Division. She was an author, director of the NAACP Legal Defense Fund, and law professor at the University of Pennsylvania. In her book *The Tyranny of the Majority* she chronicled how the numerical minority status of black voters deprives them of democracy. They are unable to see the policies they support put into effect unless white people also support those policies. Black candidates to high office cannot win unless they distance themselves from the political aspirations of the black community.

Her thesis was easily provable, but the ferocity of attacks on Guinier was prodigious. Republicans were determined to undo her nomination by calling her crazy and making fun of her hairstyle and even her name. She was disparaged as the "quota queen," despite her opposition to quotas, in a not-subtle resurrection of Ronald Reagan's mythic "welfare queen." Even supposedly liberal outlets like *The New York Times* jumped on the bandwagon of attacking Guinier, saying, "Without question the nominee herself created the basic problem."[6] The Clinton administration did not allow Guinier to defend herself but refused to defend her, either. After weeks of allowing her to twist in the wind, the nomination was withdrawn.

The Guinier character assassination wasn't the end of Clinton's obeisance to racism to achieve political ends. In 1994 he signed the

Violent Crime Control and Law Enforcement Act, which began the disastrous escalation of mass incarceration of black people. Draconian sentences imposed for the distribution of crack cocaine were part of that law. Thousands of people still languish in jail for what were once considered minor offenses.

Even after sucker-punching black political figures at their own events, disavowing qualified nominees, and putting more black people in jail, Clinton wasn't finished. He came into office in 1992 with Democratic majorities in both houses of Congress. In 1994 the Republicans swept them out of power, and the man with little conviction began throwing his constituents under the bus. Welfare reform became the main means of doing so. His mantra "end welfare as we know it" evoked every stereotype about poor Americans, who are often assumed to be black. The Personal Responsibility and Work Opportunity Reconciliation Act of 1996 put limits on cash grants, gave the states greater leeway in administering public assistance, and enacted requirements that the food stamp program be digitized. This last requirement created a lucrative system of corporate welfare, which continues to this day. Private corporations administer SNAP benefits for all fifty states.[7] Poverty became a profit center because of Clinton.

Despite the years of insults and punishments he inflicted on them, most black voters still supported Clinton. No matter how bad Democrats were, black people clung to them like life vests after a shipwreck. Frederick Douglass had said of the Republicans, "The Republican Party is the ship and all else is the sea around us."[8] The role as white people's party had shifted a hundred years later, and it was the Democrats who were perceived as providing refuge from disaster, even when they created conditions that impacted black people in such negative ways.

GEORGE W. BUSH

2001–2009

The forty-third president of the United States came to office not by popular vote but through victory in the Electoral College. This mechanism had elected Rutherford B. Hayes in 1876, but over the next 124 years Americans were assured that a repeat of this scenario was remote — until Election Day in 2000.

George W. Bush won the state of Florida because his brother, Governor Jeb Bush, issued policies that took thousands of black voters, almost all Democrats, off the voter rolls. Florida prevented former felons from voting, and under Governor Bush's direction the state undertook a massive campaign that claimed many eligible voters were felons and thus ineligible. Between fifty-seven and ninety-one thousand people were purged from the voter rolls, most of them erroneously.[1] Much was made of "hanging chads" — partially punched ballots that could nonetheless be deemed invalid — and the Supreme Court case *Bush v. Gore* decided the election on that basis. Black voter suppression, taken straight from the Reconstruction-era playbook, won the day. Bush the younger became president because the power of anti-black racism had not abated.

Bush entered office as an unpopular man, with more than half the country opposing him. He had the good political fortune of serving in office on September 11, 2001, when a terrorist attack killed three thousand people in New York City, Washington, DC, and Pennsylvania. A compliant corporate media rallied around him and didn't ask hard questions about how the attack could have taken place at all. The result was that a man widely considered unprepared for the presidency and subpar intellectually wound up serving two terms in office.

George W. Bush benefited from having aides who knew how to make him and the Republican Party appear less racist. The goal was to diminish black turnout and perhaps get votes from middle-of-the-road whites. Bush famously brought black faces to political conventions and other venues to ameliorate the racism that his party had stoked. But all was for naught in August 2005 when Hurricane Katrina struck New Orleans and the Gulf Coast.

The federal government was unprepared as the levees failed and New Orleans was flooded. Residents who couldn't leave were stranded, and the iconic city took on the look of what is commonly called the third world. More than two thousand people died, and the unresponsive federal government was blamed for the human catastrophe. All the photo ops did him little good; as Kanye West famously said, "George W. Bush doesn't care about black people." That assessment was popularly thought to be true, and putting black people in photos no longer impressed anyone.

Even before the Katrina disaster Bush received a negligible number of black votes, just like every other post-civil-rights-era Republican. However, he did prepare the country for the possibility of a black president with two major appointments to his cabinet. He appointed Condoleeza Rice as national security adviser. And former general Colin Powell, who had held that position previously, was confirmed as secretary of state. There had never been two such highly placed black people in any administration. Powell in particular was greatly admired by black people and had briefly considered running for president himself. The two played a role in every major foreign policy decision and were lauded by most other black people because of it. Their presence not only served to bring black pride to an otherwise reviled administration, but it also began the process of ending black America's left-leaning foreign policy positions.

Black Americans had historically mistrusted white America's foreign policy rationales and openly respected and admired some world leaders, such as Fidel Castro, who were considered the nation's enemies. Black Americans had held him in high regard despite censure by politicians and the corporate media. That tradition of independent thought was severely curtailed by the sight of Powell and Rice executing foreign policy decisions for a Republican president.

When Colin Powell addressed the United Nations claiming that satellite photos of trucks proved that Iraqi president Saddam Hussein was manufacturing chemical weapons, black Americans continued to support him personally, despite their disapproval of the 2003 invasion that followed his speech. Excuses ran the gamut from the argument that he was "only doing his job" to fanciful claims that he was like the character "The Spook Who Sat by the Door," trusted by white people but secretly plotting revolution. Powell was in fact a careerist who had made inroads with powerful Republicans. Reagan's defense secretary, Caspar Weinberger, was a mentor of Powell's and landed him a national security adviser position late in the Reagan administration.

Rice also rose to prominence as a result of connections with powerful Republicans. George H. W. Bush had appointed her to a staff position on the National Security Council. The initial public pronouncements were glowing. She was an accomplished pianist and former figure skater who spoke French and Russian. She was a true believer in the Republican Party and had famously stated that civil rights would have come to the United States without mass political agitation and that "segregation had become not just a real moral problem, but it had become a real pain in the neck for white people."[2] History shows that white people had violently defended segregation. The "pain in the neck" was entirely a Rice invention.

The Powell and Rice foreign policy team behaved as all their predecessors had in promoting American hegemony around the world. In 2001 they both said that Saddam Hussein had been contained, neutered, and defanged. "He has not developed any significant capability with respect to weapons of mass destruction. He is unable to project conventional power against his neighbors," Powell declared. Rice added for good measure, "We are able to keep his arms from him. His military forces have not been rebuilt." Those words went straight down the proverbial memory hole after September 11. Bush used the al-Qaeda attacks to make good on the Iraqi regime change project that neo-conservatives had long wanted.

Powell and Rice went right along with Bush. They prepared black America to expect black people in high places to act as their white counterparts did. They made it easier to forget the political left consensus that had long held sway among black people. If Colin Powell could come close to running for president and then make the case for aggression and war crimes committed by a Republican, supporting a black commander in chief was a logical progression.

BARACK OBAMA

2009–2017

While black Americans engaged in endless debate about whether they would ever live to see a black president, only a few thoughtful people asked if that prospect would be worthwhile. The office itself has furthered the racist project ever since the country's founding. Presidents have either been openly bigoted or proved to be fairweather friends ready to stand in solidarity with anti-black racism whenever doing so became politically expedient.

Barack Obama's ascension to the office and his actions in it prove that the history and practice of politics are weighted against black people in this country. He won election after the concentration of wealth and power of the group known colloquially as "the 1 percent" weighed in heavily. The people of the US typically have no voice in the presidential selection process until it is well under way. Before any ballots are cast in Iowa or New Hampshire, the ruling classes hold a "casting call" of prospective candidates and give their thumbs up or down. There was no exception for Barack Obama. In fact, as a black person he was scrutinized even more closely to make sure he would not veer off the prescribed path to the highest political office in the land.

The rules of being a "serious" candidate go something like this: Don't make rich people angry. Don't make white people angry. Don't appear to help black people in any way, because that gets white people angrier than just about anything else. Obama knew this, but he was also instinctively a conservative man, which he said to anyone who was really paying attention. During his first campaign in 2008 he spoke lovingly of Ronald Reagan as a "transformative"[1] political figure. The biracial child of a Kenyan father who had abandoned him, Obama never passed up a chance to lambaste black men as if they all were the father he hardly knew. On Father's Day and in a black church no less, Obama gave credence to the most damaging myths about black men: "But if we are honest with ourselves, we'll admit that what too many fathers also are is missing — missing from too many lives and too many homes. They have abandoned their responsibilities, acting like boys instead of men. And the foundations of our families are weaker because of it. You and I know how true this is in the African-American community."[2] If Hillary Clinton, his competitor for the Democratic nomination, had made a remark about absent black fathers she would have been rightly called a racist. Obama was so celebrated that he could get away with any words, no matter how harmful. On the other hand, his white predecessors had already benefited from the belief that Democrats could do no wrong. His dismissive words were part of a long and ignominious tradition of black voters clinging desperately to whichever party claimed to work in their interests.

Obama often managed to do what no one else could. He even succeeded in disparaging his former church pastor, the United Church of Christ's Reverend Jeremiah Wright. Wright is a firebrand who takes no prisoners in speaking the truth about American history. But when his past statements, such as "God damn America" for the country's treatment of its citizens, became known, the candidate disassociated himself from his former pastor. Obama described the well-respected minister as being "wrong and divisive," an old man who lived in the past and whose words "amplify the negative."[3] Such scorn directed toward clergy is generally not acceptable among black people. But if Bill Clinton could use Sister Souljah, Obama could publicly castigate his former minister without paying a political price.

Obama was a shrewd politician with an excellent marketing team behind him. His slogan of bringing "hope and change" struck a chord and inspired millions to support him; even those who had previously been disengaged politically became Obama enthusiasts. Hillary Clinton was considered the front-runner, but Obama's acumen made the race more competitive than anyone had expected, and he emerged as the nominee.

When Obama was elected to the Senate in 2004, America had a number of black politicians but very little in the way of black politics. In his speech at that year's Democratic convention he said, "There is no white America, there is no black America." This seemingly idealistic, historically absurd statement was in fact a clear political manifesto. Obama was making the case to white people that there would be no agenda resurrecting black politics, either. Black people were just overjoyed to witness his ascension and gave him a pass.

Black voters are often among the most left-leaning of all Democrats, but their politics can be modified by two things: the fear of Republican victory and the desire to support black candidates for office. Obama was unfamiliar to most black voters around the country. They knew little about him; some feared that his mixed-race ancestry and parentage from another country gave him no connection with themselves or with their lives. Others were concerned with whether white people would vote for him.

Those fears disappeared overnight when Obama emerged victorious in the Iowa caucuses in January 2008. He proved he could get white votes and that he could possibly become president of the United States. That ended any scrutiny or questioning from most black voters. They could practice support for someone perceived as one of their own without risking Republican victory. Those who dared to pose a question about Obama's candidacy were shouted down in favor of the prospect of seeing a black president. Some claimed that they would make demands of Obama after he emerged victorious. They would "hold his feet to the fire," as the saying went.

After he was elected there was, of course, no such effort. Most black Americans acted like thirty million Secret Service agents, putting themselves in the path of any criticism of their president. White racism made it difficult to critique him. Some who were disposed to pose hard questions would instead defend him lest his racist detractors succeed in bringing him down.

Barack Obama came along at the perfect moment in history for a candidate like him to win the presidential election. Black politics had been destroyed decades earlier when Martin Luther King and Malcolm X were assassinated. The Black Panthers and other revolutionaries were imprisoned or dead. The liberation movement had been destroyed by COINTELPRO, a program orchestrated at the highest levels of power in the country. Black politics came under the same pressure from the Democratic Party donor class. The rise of black politics in the Obama era was illusory, and few substantive issues were addressed.[4]

Chief among Obama's tormentors was New York real estate developer and reality show star Donald Trump. In 2010 and 2011, Trump became the face of the so-called birthers, a subset of people who believed that Obama was born in Kenya and not Hawaii and therefore ineligible under the Constitution to become president. Despite Obama providing as evidence his birth certificate and passport, Trump persisted in popularizing the racist-tinged speculation. The president ultimately chose to release a more detailed

long-form birth certificate shortly after he carried out the assassination of Osama bin Laden. The well-chosen timing ended in
public humiliation for Trump as Obama made him the butt of jokes
at the White House correspondents' dinner in 2011. At the time no
one knew that Trump would run for the Republican nomination
and become Obama's successor.

Black Americans had little but happiness to show for Obama's
two terms in office. He behaved as his Democratic predecessors
had, making white Americans' dreams come true. His solution to
the 2008 economic collapse was to bail out the financial sector.
There were no proposals for the government to step in and assist
the millions of people devastated by wrongdoing at the top.

Obama successfully marketed himself as an anti-war candidate
— but he never said anything of the kind. He said he was only
opposed to "dumb wars." That is to say, those that involved sending
US troops to fight abroad. Instead he relied on proxies as a regime
change method in Libya, Syria, and Ukraine. The US military's
Africa Command, AFRICOM, continued the American takeover
of African nations' military forces. Under the guise of fighting
terrorism Obama sent drones that killed civilians in Afghanistan,
Pakistan, and Yemen. He even killed American citizens — Anwar
al-Awlaki and his sixteen-year-old son, Abdul Rahman al-Awlaki
— via drone strikes in Yemen.

At home black people continued to be killed at disproportion-
ately high rates by members of law enforcement, one every twenty-
eight hours. The Black Lives Matter (BLM) movement came to
prominence in the last two years of Obama's presidency, but its
leaders were as squeamish about taking on Obama as the rest
of black America. There was never a connection made between
the mass movement that BLM spawned and demands for federal
government redress. Even activists handled him with kid gloves.

Ultimately, all of Obama's shortcomings were overshadowed by
the shock of Donald Trump's victory over Hillary Clinton in 2016.

The woman thought to be the favorite since the moment Obama nearly cleared the Democratic field for her by naming her his secretary of state ended up the loser. She won the popular vote but lost in a close contest decided by the Electoral College. It was an ignominious end to the first black American presidency, which revealed the hollowness of the achievement.

DONALD TRUMP

2017–

The election of Donald Trump as president of the United States is arguably the most remarkable story in the history of presidential politics. A man with no prior public service experience, who was heartily disliked by more than half of the electorate, defeated the person groomed to be Obama's successor. Hillary Clinton made good on her husband's promise of "two for the price of one" as she served in her husband's administration, became a two-term senator from New York, and was appointed secretary of state in Barack Obama's first term in office. Paradoxically, this résumé became a liability when she ran against two outsiders, Bernie Sanders in the Democratic Party primary and Donald Trump in the general election. Nor could she overcome the overt and covert racist appeals of the Trump campaign.

Donald Trump ran for office as an outsider and an outlier. He opposed free trade agreements and regime change, which were part of the elite ruling-class orthodoxy. But his signature campaign slogan, "Make America Great Again," resonated with white Americans. Even white women voted for him in greater numbers than they did for Hillary Clinton, who would have been the first female president. Although Donald Trump had never held a government or elected office, he was a well-known public figure. A real estate developer who inherited his business from his father, he used his position in a constant effort to garner publicity for himself. There was good reason to doubt Trump's claims of business success. Despite inheriting an enormous amount of money and income-producing assets, his businesses had filed for bankruptcy on six occasions, and he was better known for refusing to pay vendors and even the attorneys who defended his theft of services.[1] His father, Fred Trump, had made a fortune building moderate-income housing in Queens and Long Island and consistently discriminated against black people seeking housing. In 1927, Trump senior was arrested at a Ku Klux Klan rally, presumably as a participant.[2]

Trump's earlier forays into public activity should have disqualified him from the presidency. He was known for creating the popular reality-based series *The Apprentice* and *Celebrity Apprentice* in which he played himself dispensing with contestants with his signature line, "You're fired!" In 2011 he embarked on a failed quest to prove that Barack Obama was not born in the United States and was therefore ineligible for the presidency. Obama celebrated the release of his long-form birth certificate with a very public skewering of Trump at the 2011 White House correspondents' dinner. Obama's jokes went over well with the crowd and the media but obviously less so with Trump. "We all know about your credentials and breadth of experience. For example — no, seriously — just recently, in an episode of *Celebrity Apprentice* . . ."

But it was Trump who got the last laugh. He proved that presidential racism existed because it is so effective. During the presidential campaign Trump showed his most overt racist animus toward Mexican immigrants, charging that they were rapists and murderers and vowing to build a wall on the border at the expense of the Mexican government. This was classic American white supremacy, claiming the United States as a country for white people that needed to be made "great again."

Despite the reservations of the Republican establishment, Trump bested his rivals in the primaries and emerged as the party's nominee. He energized new voters just as Obama had, and while he lost the popular vote he won an Electoral College victory, easily defeating Clinton with the number of states in his win column.

The Democratic electoral debacle had been building for some time. Obama won the presidency and Democrats controlled the House and the Senate in 2009 and 2010, but their record for victories declined after that. In preceding years, Republicans had been gaining increasing control of governorships and legislative positions and aggressively using their power to gerrymander, redrawing legislative districts to their advantage, and created congressional and state legislative districts that became "safe seats" for Republicans. The Republicans regained control of Congress while Obama was still in office, and the presidency itself was the last domino to fall, officially making Obama's legacy an empty one.

Trump had a long history of making anti-black statements throughout his career. His references to "the blacks" and use of the long-anachronistic term *inner city* were classically racist. He paid for full-page newspaper advertisements in 1989 calling for the death penalty for black and Latino teenagers falsely accused in a headline-grabbing Central Park rape case. The teens were eventually exonerated after many years in jail, but Trump never retracted his stance, nor was it forgotten.

The same country that had made history eight years earlier by electing a black man to the presidency now elected an openly racist white man. The corporate media mocked him, but white America ran to his side. He was bulletproof: Nothing hurt his electoral success. His racist statements, charges of fascism, claims of sexual harassment, ill-informed outbursts on Twitter, and calls to ban Muslim travel and to curtail or ban immigration from countries that are predominantly non-white did nothing to stop his victory. In fact, his expressions of bigotry, both coded and overt, formed the basis of his appeal for many voters. He was inaugurated the forty-fifth president on January 20, 2017.

Within weeks of his inauguration Trump attempted to make good on his promises. With professional white supremacist Steve Bannon as his chief strategist he declared his intention to build the wall on Mexico's border. He signed an executive order banning entry to the United States by citizens of seven mostly Muslim nations: Syria, Iran, Iraq, Libya, Sudan, Somalia, and Yemen. But opinion polls showed that more Americans approved than disapproved of his presidency, even if a majority did not like him, and once again Trump's invincibility was evident. A federal judge declared the entry ban illegal, but the dire consequences of a Trump presidency were already becoming evident, and the Supreme Court would ultimately endorse his authority to implement a reworded travel ban that was not justified by any evidence or legitimate policy objectives.

Trump is simply the latest person to seize on white angst in order to win a presidential election. The combination of his open racism and the Democratic Party's failure to produce the hope and change that the Obama campaign said were coming put him in the White House. The reaction to his election split the country, with more than half of voters disliking Trump and predicting everything from a new Hitlerism to World War III.

In fact, Trump did what his predecessors did, building upon the actions of the prior administration. The seven nations chosen for the travel ban were subjected to actual military attack or brutal economic and diplomatic sanctions during the Obama years. American drones and sanctions created humanitarian crises in these countries. Trump did what Obama may have wanted but dared not do: He brought these attacks to the fore of American political discourse. Even liberals who turned a blind eye to Obama's war-making could not avert their eyes to illegality and mistreatment in their home communities.

Trump is an anomaly in some ways, but he shares a long pattern of racism with his forty-three predecessors. Donald Trump certainly knows his people. He understands white voters better than the Republican Party establishment did. But he doesn't understand much else, and his presidency is in serious danger as a result of his public fights with anyone who doesn't support him without question. Republican congressional leaders are as likely to face his wrath as a journalist who attacks him.

The Republican establishment may not have wanted Trump to be president, but ultimately they benefited from a long history of anti-black political campaigns. He is a rogue, attacking the bipartisan neo-liberal consensus on trade and foreign policy. He actually proved that Republican ideology was less important to white America than their sense of entitlement and their expectation of being catered to by the political system. Black people are horrified when it is obvious that he doesn't know who Frederick Douglass was, but his supporters certainly don't care. He is as ill-informed a president as he showed himself to be during his campaign. It is Making (white) America Great Again that matters the most to him and to the American public who elected him.

The Democratic Party was shocked by Hillary Clinton's defeat and cannot agree on a way to fight Trump. Trump is the nightmare, the open racist who gets support precisely for that reason. Now the black political leadership is lost; aside from committing themselves to fighting Trump, their allegiance to and reliance on the hapless Democratic Party has neutered them. The triumphant racist has no reason to fear black people or what passes for leadership. The most recent American president has taken black people back to the first.

Trump presents many contradictions. The gloves are off, the code words are gone. He is a unique personality in the modern presidency: a man without any discernible social graces. When he referred to the global south as comprising "shithole countries" in an Oval Office meeting, at least one meeting participant broke the rules of protocol and publicly disclosed the remark.

Trump's open racism is a threat to black people. Racist Americans feel empowered and emboldened. In August 2017, just months after the Trump inauguration, they converged on Charlottesville, Virginia, and in the clashes between white supremacists and counterprotesters one woman was killed when a Trump supporter drove his car into a crowd. The president refused to condemn the white supremacists, saying that there were "fine people on both sides."[3]

Trump is no anomaly. He appears at the recent end of a continuum that began with a series of slaveholders. The nation's capital was created to ensure its safety among the slaveholding states. While Trump's demeanor makes him seem like an outlier, history proves that he is not.

EPILOGUE

Presidential historians love their subject matter. Research for this book revealed a massive burying of the truth by acclaimed scholars and presidents' biographers. Lincoln's approval of the Île à Vache colony is not a secret. Anyone who researches him knows this to be true; it is a fact that's easy to prove. Yet those who love Lincoln want to deny the truth and maintain a positive, one-sided perspective about the object of their admiration, and so they omit this information from their carefully curated biographies.

Martin Luther King, Jr., famously said, "Injustice anywhere is a threat to justice everywhere... Whatever affects one directly, affects all indirectly." This maxim has implications for how we write, read, and think about history and about our conduct in the present day. Apologists tend to excuse slaveholders as "products of their time" and to elide their moral failings when celebrating their accomplishments. Yet slavery was rendered no less evil and the suffering of the enslaved was made no less painful by the fact that their perpetrators were acting lawfully and in accordance with societal norms. Every life is of equal value, and actions that can only be tolerated when victims are regarded to some degree as "the other" — whether it's sending other people's children to inadequate public schools or killing wedding guests with smart bombs in Afghanistan — need to be viewed and talked about with honesty. Truth-telling has to start somewhere, and a full, clear-eyed accounting of presidential history is as good a place to start as any.

American presidents bought and sold human beings, terrorized indigenous people and drove them from their native land, and waged wars of aggression against other nations. When they have done good it was often because they were pressured by the actions of the people and not because they were inclined to do right. Yet these former leaders are consistently described as shrewd and brilliant. They are praised for violating the most basic precepts of universally accepted morality. Jacksonian democracy was an effort to extend slaveholding to a larger population. Compromises that were praised as politically necessary ended up extending the cruelty of slavery until it could only be stopped by a four-year-long war.

Presidents were openly racist and caved to the demands of the most retrograde forces in society. Criticism is reserved for those who failed politically or were disgraced or lost reelection campaigns. Rough riders and Indian fighters are idolized and turned into heroes when they were nothing more than mass killers with good public relations teams behind them. Barack Obama was falsely sold as a peace-seeking candidate, but he claimed and exercised a previously unknown right to kill Americans overseas without charge or trial. Moreover, he presided over the dramatically expanded use of unmanned drones to assassinate foreign nationals, killing untold numbers of innocents — so-called "collateral damage" — in the process. His political skill and "Teflon" popularity put him beyond scrutiny.

Donald Trump is vilified because his open racism tarnishes the brand. The system depends upon its capacity to make people feel good about their country and themselves. Trump makes that difficult, instead embarrassing people who want to have positive feelings about their government. What was once a dark underbelly is now the very face of the US government.

Trump's racism gives people who previously kept their opinions private a certain level of comfort. Now they have no reason to hide and, in fact, are encouraged to flaunt their ideology. On August 12, 2017, a group of white supremacists gathered in Charlottesville, Virginia, to protest the planned removal of a monument dedicated to Confederate general Robert E. Lee. The march was not confined to support for Confederate monuments. Armed militia accompanied self-proclaimed racists and white supremacists.

Donald Trump's election was a catalyst for these protests, and he won the election because he reads white Americans so well. He is the everyman, albeit wealthier. He says what they say: "President George Washington was a slave owner, so will George Washington lose his status? Are we gonna take down statues of George Washington? How about Thomas Jefferson? What do you think of Thomas Jefferson? Do you like him? Because he was a major slave owner too. Are we gonna take down his statue?"

A *New York Times* reader survey, hardly the typical source for proof of Trump support, demonstrated the reluctance of white Americans to jettison their beloved Founding Fathers. A mere 4 percent approved of removing a statue of George Washington. White supremacy is not usually expressed explicitly. Admiration of terrible people is an expression of support for the colonial settler project, no matter how the admirer may justify the sentiment.

This book is an effort to expose America's sordid history. The liars and obfuscators have held sway for four hundred years. Cowardice and passivity have held sway for too long. It is time for the truth-tellers to come forward. They must do so fearlessly, knowing that most of their countrymen and -women still don't want to remove a statue of George Washington. If Americans can ask Germans to apologize for the Holocaust or ponder why Joseph Stalin is still popular in Russia, they can be told to cast Andrew Jackson from the twenty-dollar bill and from any notion of respectability.

NOTES

Preface

1. W. E. B. Du Bois, "I Won't Vote," *The Nation*, October 20, 1956, https://www.thenation.com/article/i-wont-vote.
2. Gerald Horne, *The Counter-Revolution of 1776: Slave Resistance and the Origins of the United States of America* (New York: New York University Press, 2014), 211.

Chapter 1: George Washington

1. Mary V. Thompson, "The Private Life of George Washington's Slaves," accessed December 31, 2016, http://www.pbs.org/wgbh/pages/frontline/shows/jefferson/video/lives.html.
2. "Founders Online: From George Washington to Tobias Lear, 12 April 1791," accessed December 31, 2016, http://founders.archives.gov/documents/Washington/05-08-02-0062.
3. "The President's House: Interview with Oney Judge," accessed December 31, 2016, http://www.ushistory.org/presidentshouse/slaves/oneyinterview.php.
4. Fritz Hirschfeld, *George Washington and Slavery: A Documentary Portrayal* (Columbia and London: University of Missouri Press, 1997), 113.
5. John C. Fitzpatrick (ed.), *The Writings of George Washington from the Original Manuscript Sources 1745–1799*, vol. 34: *October 11, 1794–March 29, 1796* (Washington, DC: Government Printing Office, 1939), 48.
6. Booker T. Washington, *Up from Slavery: An Autobiography* (New York: Doubleday, Page, 1907), 34.
7. Hirschfeld, *George Washington and Slavery*, 214.

Chapter 2: John Adams

1. Frederic Kidder, *History of the Boston Massacre, March 5, 1770; Consisting of the Narrative of the Town, the Trial of the Soldiers: And a Historical Introduction, Containing Unpublished Documents of John Adams, and Explanatory Notes* (Albany, NY: Joel Munsell, 1870), 258, http://hdl.handle.net/2027/mdp.39015008486659.
2. Arthur Scherr, *John Adams, Slavery, and Race: Ideas, Politics, and Diplomacy in an Age of Crisis* (Santa Barbara and Denver: Praeger, 2018), 30.
3. *The Works of John Adams, Second President of the United States*, vol. 9: *Letters and State Papers 1799–1811* (Boston: Little, Brown, 1854), 93.
4. *The Works of John Adams*, vol. 9, 92.
5. *The Works of John Adams*, vol. 9, 92.
6. "Founders Online: From John Adams to Henry Colman, 13 January 1817," accessed December 31, 2016, http://founders.archives.gov/documents/Adams/99-02-02-6692.
7. "Founders Online: From John Adams to Henry Colman, 13 January 1817."
8. "April 15 1814: John Adams Explains Everything," *Pastnow* (blog), April 16, 2014, https://pastnow.wordpress.com/2014/04/15/april-15-1814-john-adams-explains-everything.
9. Scherr, *John Adams, Slavery, and Race*, 152.
10. "Founders Online: From John Adams to William Tudor, Jr., 1 December 1819," accessed January 6, 2019, http://founders.archives.gov/documents/Adams/99-02-02-7273.

Chapter 3: Thomas Jefferson

1. Joseph J. Ellis, *American Creation: Triumphs and Tragedies at the Founding of the Republic* (New York: Vintage Books, 2008), 240.
2. Ben Kiernan, *Blood and Soil: A World History of Genocide and Extermination from Sparta to Darfur* (New Haven, CT, and London: Yale University Press, 2007), 328.
3. Merrill D. Peterson, (ed.), *Visitors to Monticello* (Charlottesville: University Press of Virginia, 1989), 90–91.
4. Gary B. Nash and Graham Russell Hodges, *Friends of Liberty: Thomas Jefferson, Tadeusz Kościuszko, and Agrippa Hull: A Tale of Three Patriots, Two Revolutions, and a Tragic Betrayal of Freedom in the New Nation* (New York: Basic Books, 2008), 163.
5. Nash and Hodges, *Friends of Liberty*, 164.

Chapter 4: James Madison

1. Drew R. McCoy, *The Last of the Fathers: James Madison and the Republican Legacy* (Cambridge, UK: Cambridge University Press, 1991), 318.
2. McCoy, *The Last of the Fathers*, 320.
3. "Equality: James Madison, Memorandum on an African Colony for Freed Slaves," accessed April 14, 2019, http://press-pubs.uchicago.edu/founders/documents/v1ch15s43.html.
4. Charles A. Nelson, *Back to Africa? The Solution to America's Race Problem as Viewed by Jefferson, Madison, Clay, and Lincoln* (Bloomington, IN: Xlibris, 2009), 24.
5. Kurt E. Leichtle and Bruce Carveth, *Crusade Against Slavery: Edward Coles, Pioneer of Freedom* (Carbondale and Edwardsville: Southern Illinois University Press, 2011), 69.

Chapter 5: James Monroe

1. "Monroe Slave Census," accessed December 31, 2016, http://www.leesburgva.gov/home/showdocument?id=8851.
2. Thomas Hart Benton, *Thirty Years' View: Or, A History of the Working of the American Government for Thirty Years, from 1820 to 1850. Chiefly Taken from the Congress Debates, the Private Papers of General Jackson, and the Speeches of Ex-Senator Benton, with His Actual View of Men and Affairs; with Historical Notes and Illustrations, and Some Notices of Eminent Deceased Contemporaries* (New York: D. Appleton, 1883), 170.
3. "Jackson's Infamous Execution of Two British Citizens During the War," *Rebellion: John Horse and the Black Seminoles, the First Black Rebels to Beat American Slavery* (website), accessed December 31, 2016, http://www.johnhorse.com/trail/01/b/24.1.htm.
4. Nero James Pruitt, *The Forty-Three Presidents: What They Said To and About Each Other* (Bloomington, IN: iUniverse, 2015), 245.
5. "James Monroe: Seventh Annual Message," accessed April 9, 2017, http://www.presidency.ucsb.edu/ws/?pid=29465.
6. John Bolton, interview by Jake Tapper, CNN, March 3, 2019.

Chapter 6: John Quincy Adams

1. Paul C. Nagel, *John Quincy Adams: A Public Life, a Private Life* (Cambridge, MA: Harvard University Press, 1999), 386.
2. Genealogy Bank (website), accessed April 15, 2017, https://www.genealogybank.com/doc/newspapers/image/v2%3A109E2A3EA01155D8%40GB3NEWS-1428391D39829478%402392888-1426E7F73093DE08%401-14324AEF219C0BAA%40Letter%2BII?search_terms=john%7cadams%7cabolition.
3. Charles Francis Adams (ed.), *Memoirs of John Quincy Adams: Comprising Portions of His Diary from 1795 to 1848*, Volume IV (Philadelphia: J. B. Lippincott, 1875), 503.

4. "The Senate Debate on the Breckenridge Bill for the Government of Louisiana, 1804," in John Franklin Jameson, Henry Eldridge Bourne, and Robert Livingston Schuyler (eds.), *The American Historical Review*, vol. 22, No. 2: *October 1916 to July 1917* (London: Macmillan, 1917), 346.

Chapter 7: Andrew Jackson

1. Melvin Steinfield, *Our Racist Presidents: From Washington to Nixon* (San Ramon, CA: Consensus Publishers, 1972), 80.
2. "*Worcester v. Georgia* 31 U.S. 515 (1832)," Justia (website), accessed April 30, 2017, https://supreme.justia.com/cases/federal/us/31/515/case.html.
3. Steinfield, *Our Racist Presidents*, 81.
4. "December 3 1814: To the Free Colored Inhabitants of Louisiana," *Pastnow* (blog), December 3, 2014, https://pastnow.wordpress.com/2014/12/03/december-3-1814-to-the -free-colored-inhabitants-of-louisiana.
5. Merton L Dillon, *Slavery Attacked: Southern Slaves and Their Allies 1619–1865* (Baton Rouge and London: Louisiana State University Press, 1990), 82.
6. "Treasury Secretary Lew Announces Front of New $20 to Feature Harriet Tubman, Lays Out Plans for New $20, $10 and $5," accessed June 15, 2019, https://www.treasury.gov/press-center/press-releases/Pages/jl0436.aspx.
7. Jim Webb, "We Can Celebrate Harriet Tubman Without Disparaging Andrew Jackson," *Washington Post*, April 24, 2016, https://www.washingtonpost.com/opinions/we-can -celebrate-harriet-tubman-without-disparaging-andrew-jackson/2016/04/24/2f766160 -0894-11e6-a12f-ea5aed7958dc_story.html?utm_term=.ffaf10386bd6.

Chapter 8: Martin Van Buren

1. Bob Navarro, *The Era of Change: Executives and Events in a Period of Rapid Expansion* (Bloomington, IN: Xlibris, 2006), 78.
2. William G. Shade, "'The Most Delicate and Exciting Topics': Martin Van Buren, Slavery, and the Election of 1836," *Journal of the Early Republic* 18, no. 3 (1998): 478, https://doi .org/10.2307/3124674.
3. Christoper Brian Booker, *The Black Presidential Nightmare: African-Americans and Presidents, 1789–2016* (Bloomington, IN: Xlibris, 2017), 108.
4. Donald B. Cole, *Martin Van Buren and the American Political System* (Princeton, NJ: Princeton University Press, 2016), 270.
5. Martin Van Buren, "State of the Union Address," December 5, 1837, https://www .infoplease.com/homework-help/us-documents/state-union-address-martin-van -buren-december-5-1837.
6. Cole, *Martin van Buren and the American Political System*, 363.
7. Michael J. Gerhardt, *The Forgotten Presidents: Their Untold Constitutional Legacy* (New York: Oxford University Press, 2013), 14.

Chapter 9: William Henry Harrison

1. Republican Committee of 76, *The Northern Man with Southern Principles, and the Southern Man with American Principles: Or a View of the Comparative Claims of Gen. William H. Harrison and Martin Van Buren, Esq., Candidates for the Presidency, to the Support of Citizens of the Southern States* (1840), 19.
2. Republican Committee of 76, *The Northern Man with Southern Principles*, 20.

Chapter 10: John Tyler

1. Robert John Walker and YA Pamphlet Collection (Library of Congress), *Letter of Mr. Walker, of Mississippi, Relative to the Annexation of Texas: In Reply to the Call of the*

People of Carroll County, Kentucky, to Communicate His Views on That Subject (Washington, DC: Printed at the Globe Office, 1844), http://archive.org/details/letterofmrwalker00walk.

Chapter 11: James K. Polk

1. John O'Sullivan, "Annexation (1845)," August 1845, https://pdcrodas.webs.ull.es/anglo/OSullivanAnnexation.pdf.
2. William Dusinberre, *Slavemaster President: The Double Career of James Polk*, 1st ed. (New York: Oxford University Press, 2007), 130.
3. Dusinberre, *Slavemaster President*, 142.
4. David Wilmot, "Speech of Mr. Wilmot, of Pennsylvania, on His Amendment Restricting Slavery from Territory Hereafter Acquired: Delivered in the House of Representatives of the United States, Feb. 8, 1847," http://archive.org/details/ASPC0005059800.

Chapter 12: Zachary Taylor

1. K. Jack Bauer, *Zachary Taylor: Soldier, Planter, Statesman of the Old Southwest* (Baton Rouge: Louisiana State University Press, 1993), 4.
2. Bauer, *Zachary Taylor*, 108.
3. Frederick Merk and Lois Bannister Merk, *Manifest Destiny and Mission in American History: A Reinterpretation* (Cambridge, MA: Harvard University Press, 1963), 1995.
4. Jefferson Davis, *The Papers of Jefferson Davis July 1846 – December 1848* (Baton Rouge: Louisiana State University Press, 1981), 307.

Chapter 13: Millard Fillmore

1. Frank H. Severance (ed.), *Millard Fillmore Papers*, vol. 1 (Buffalo, NY: Buffalo Historical Society, 1907), 322.

Chapter 14: Franklin Pierce

1. Walter Johnson, *River of Dark Dreams: Slavery and Empire in the Cotton Kingdom* (Cambridge, MA: Harvard University Press, 2013), 366.
2. Johnson, *River of Dark Dreams*, 322.
3. John Alexander Logan, *The Great Conspiracy: What Led Us to the Civil War* (Civil War Classics) (New York: Diversion Books, 2015), 318.

Chapter 15: James Buchanan

1. "James Buchanan: Inaugural Address," accessed March 12, 2017, https://www.presidency.ucsb.edu/documents/inaugural-address-33.
2. Philip Shriver Klein, *President James Buchanan: A Biography* (Newtown, CT: American Political Biography Press, 1995), 269.
3. Barry Friedman, *The Will of the People: How Public Opinion Has Influenced the Supreme Court and Shaped the Meaning of the Constitution* (New York: Farrar, Straus and Giroux, 2009), 437.
4. Friedman, *The Will of the People*, 437.

Chapter 16: Abraham Lincoln

1. Phillip W. Magness, "The Île à Vache: From Hope to Disaster," Opinionator, https://opinionator.blogs.nytimes.com/2013/04/12/the-le-vache-from-hope-to-disaster.
2. Adam Goodheart, "How Slavery Really Ended in America," *New York Times*, April 1, 2011, http://www.nytimes.com/2011/04/03/magazine/mag-03CivilWar-t.html.
3. Howard Zinn, Kathy Emery, and Ellen Reeves, *A People's History of the United States: Abridged Teaching Edition* (New York: New Press, 2003), 140.
4. "The Colonization of People of African Descent: Interview with President Lincoln," *New-York Tribune*, August 15, 1862, accessed February 18, 2017, http://www.newspapers

.com/image/78345697/?terms=the%2Bcolonization%2Bof%2Bpeople%2Bof%2B
african%2Bdescent.

5. Lerone Bennett, *Forced into Glory: Abraham Lincoln's White Dream* (Chicago: Johnson, 2000), 453.

6. "Address on Colonization to a Deputation of Negroes," August 14, 1862, https://quod.lib .umich.edu/l/lincoln/lincoln5/1:812?rgn=div1;view=fulltext.

7. Gideon Welles, *The History of Emancipation* (New York: s.n., 1872), 848.

8. Benjamin Butler, *Butler's Book: Autobiography and Personal Reminiscences of Major-General Benjamin F. Butler: A Review of His Legal, Political, and Military Career* (Boston: A. M. Thayer, 1892), 903.

9. "Abraham Lincoln: Second Inaugural Address," March 4, 1865.

Chapter 17: Andrew Johnson

1. John Cimprich, "Military Governor Johnson and Tennessee Blacks, 1862–65," *Tennessee Historical Quarterly* 39, no. 4 (1980): 464.

2. Cimprich, "Military Governor Johnson and Tennessee Blacks," 466.

3. Annette Gordon-Reed, *Andrew Johnson: The 17th President, 1865–1869* (American Presidents Series) (New York: Macmillan, 2011), 115–16.

4. Frederick Douglass, *The Life and Times of Frederick Douglass: His Early Life as a Slave, His Escape from Bondage, and His Complete History* (Mineola, NY: Dover Publications, 2003), 264.

5. Booker, *The Black Presidential Nightmare*, 247.

6. Booker, *The Black Presidential Nightmare*, 248.

Chapter 18: Ulysses S. Grant

1. John F. Marszalek (ed.), *The Best Writings of Ulysses S. Grant* (Carbondale: Southern Illinois University Press, 2015), 12.

2. Brooks Simpson, *Ulysses S. Grant: Triumph Over Adversity, 1822–1865* (Minneapolis: Voyageur Press, 2014), 67.

3. "Ulysses S. Grant: Inaugural Address." Accessed July 10, 2019. https://www.presidency .ucsb.edu/documents/inaugural-address-37.

Chapter 19: Rutherford B. Hayes

1. Vincent P. De Santis, "The Republican Party and the Southern Negro, 1877–1897," *Journal of Negro History* 45, no. 2 (1960): 78, https://doi.org/10.2307/2716571.

2. T. Harry Williams (ed.), *Hayes: The Diary of a President: Covering the Disputed Election, the End of Reconstruction, and the Beginning of Civil Service* (New York: David McKay, 1964), 221.

Chapter 20: James A. Garfield

1. Booker, *The Black Presidential Nightmare*, 291.

2. Booker, *The Black Presidential Nightmare*, 291.

3. Allan Peskin, *Garfield: A Biography* (Kent, OH: Kent State University Press, 1978), 177.

4. Justus D. Doenecke, *The Presidencies of James A. Garfield and Chester A. Arthur* (Lawrence, Kansas: Regents Press of Kansas, 1981), 48.

5. Eric Foner, *Reconstruction: America's Unfinished Revolution, 1863–1877*, updated ed. (New York: HarperPerennial, 2014), 114.

Chapter 21: Chester A. Arthur

1. George Sinkler, *The Racial Attitudes of American Presidents from Abraham Lincoln to Theodore Roosevelt* (Garden City, NY: Doubleday, 1971), 212.

2. Stanley Hirshson, *Farewell to the Bloody Shirt: Northern Republicans and the Southern Negro, 1877–1893* (Chicago: Quadrangle, 1968), 105.

3. Chester Arthur, *State Papers, Etc., Etc., Etc., of Chester A. Arthur, President of the United States* (Washington, DC: Government Printing Office, 1885), 225.

4. Hirshson, *Farewell to the Bloody Shirt*, 107.

5. Rayford Whittingham Logan, *The Betrayal of the Negro, from Rutherford B. Hayes to Woodrow Wilson*, 1st Da Capo Press ed. (New York: Da Capo Press, 1997), 45.

Chapter 22: Grover Cleveland

1. "Grover Cleveland: A Powerful Advocate of White Supremacy," *Journal of Blacks in Higher Education*, no. 31 (2001): 54, https://doi.org/10.2307/2679168.

2. Hirshson, *Farewell to the Bloody Shirt*, 240.

3. T. Thomas Fortune, "Good Advice to the Negroes," *Memphis Daily Appeal*, November 25, 1884, https://chroniclingamerica.loc.gov/lccn/sn83045160/1884-11-25/ed-1/seq-1.pdf.

Chapter 23: Benjamin Harrison

1. Lew Wallace and Murat Halstead, *Life and Public Services of Hon. Benjamin Harrison, President of the U.S.: With a Concise Biographical Sketch of Hon. Whitelaw Reid, Ex-Minister to France* (N.p.: Edgewood Publishing: 1892), 104.

2. Wallace and Halstead, *Life and Public Services of Hon. Benjamin Harrison*, 278.

3. George Sinkler, "Benjamin Harrison and the Matter of Race." Indiana Magazine of History 65, no. 3 (September 1969): 198, https://www.jstor.org/stable/27789595.

4. Edward Frantz, "A March of Triumph? Benjamin Harrison's Southern Tour and the Limits of Racial and Regional Reconciliation," *Indiana Magazine of History* 100, no. 4 (2004): 302.

Chapter 24: Grover Cleveland

1. James A. Henretta, Kevin J. Fernlund, and Melvin Yazawa, *Documents for America's History*, vol. 2: *Since 1865* (Boston: Bedford/St. Martin's, 2011), 136.

2. Alyn Brodsky, *Grover Cleveland: A Study in Character* (New York: St. Martin's Press, 2000), 450.

3. Albert Ellery Bergh (ed.), *Letters and Addresses of Grover Cleveland* (New York: Unit Book Publishing, 1909), 425.

Chapter 25: William McKinley

1. Jennifer C. James, *A Freedom Bought with Blood: African American War Literature from the Civil War to World War II* (Chapel Hill: University of North Carolina Press, 2007), 135.

2. George P. Marks (ed.), *The Black Press Views American Imperialism (1898–1900)* (New York: Arno Press, 1971), 109.

3. Daryl Rasuli, "James B. Parker Revisited," accessed January 1, 2017, https://digital.lib .buffalo.edu/items/show/91880.

4. Deborah Davis, *Guest of Honor: Booker T. Washington, Theodore Roosevelt, and the White House Dinner That Shocked a Nation* (New York: Simon & Schuster, 2013), 132.

5. Mitch Kachun, "'Big Jim' Parker and the Assassination of William McKinley: Patriotism, Nativism, Anarchism, and the Struggle for African American Citizenship," *Journal of the Gilded Age and Progressive Era* 9, no. 1 (2010): 96.

6. Kachun, "'Big Jim' Parker and the Assassination of William McKinley," 100.

Chapter 26: Theodore Roosevelt

1. "Documents for In-Class Exam: Hist 118," 3, accessed March 3, 2019, https://wcm1.web .rice.edu/pdf/hist118-exam2-in-class.pdf.

2. "Thedore 'Teddy' Roosevelt," *Great Minds on Race* (blog), September 27, 2011, https:// greatmindsonrace.wordpress.com/2011/09/26/teddy-roosevelt.

3. Booker T. Washington and Victoria Earle Matthews, *Black-Belt Diamonds: Gems from the Speeches, Addresses, and Talks to Students of Booker T. Washington* (New York: Fortune and Scott, 1898), 72.

4. James A. Tinsley, "Roosevelt, Foraker, and the Brownsville Affray," *Journal of Negro History* 41, no. 1 (1956): 48, https://doi.org/10.2307/2715720.

5. Kathleen Dalton, *Theodore Roosevelt: A Strenuous Life* (New York: Knopf Doubleday Publishing Group, 2007), 322.

6. *San Francisco Call*, January 29, 1907, California Digital Newspaper Collection, accessed June 24, 2017, https://cdnc.ucr.edu/cgi-bin/cdnc?a=d&d=SFC19070129.2.24.

7. "Theodore Roosevelt: Sixth Annual Message," December 3, 1906, https://www.presidency.ucsb.edu/documents/sixth-annual-message-4.

8. Louis R. Harlan, *Booker T. Washington: The Wizard of Tuskegee, 1901–1915* (New York: Oxford University Press, 1986), 319.

9. Harlan, *Booker T. Washington*, 311.

10. Harlan, *Booker T. Washington*, 325.

Chapter 27: William Howard Taft

1. Horace Samuel Merrill and Marion Merrill, *The Republican Command, 1897–1913* (Lexington: University Press of Kentucky, 1971), 275.

2. Harlan, *Booker T. Washington*, 340.

3. Paul Frymer, *Uneasy Alliances: Race and Party Competition in America* (Princeton, NJ: Princeton University Press, 1999), 84.

4. "Taft Policy in South." *The Evening Star*, May 21, 1909. Accessed July 10, 2019. https://chroniclingamerica.loc.gov/lccn/sn83045462/1909-05-21/ed-1/seq-10.pdf.

Chapter 28: Woodrow Wilson

1. Alexander Walters, *My Life and Work* (New York, Chicago, Toronto, London, and Edinburgh: Fleming H. Revell, 1917), 195, accessed January 1, 2017, http://docsouth.unc.edu/neh/walters/walters.html.

2. Herbert Aptheker (ed.), *A Documentary History of the the Negro People in the United States 1910–1932* (Secaucus, NJ: Citadel Press, 1951), 77–78.

3. "Expose Roosevelt as Rabid Jim Crower," *Chicago Defender, National Edition*, October 15, 1932.

4. *The Crisis*, January 1915: 120, accessed April 30, 2017, http://library.brown.edu/pdfs/1302703938859379.pdf.

5. James Weldon Johnson, *Writings*, Library of America 145 (New York: Library of America, 2004), 610.

6. James Weldon Johnson, *Writings*, 610.

7. Charles L. Lumpkins, *American Pogrom: The East St. Louis Race Riots and Black Politics* (Athens: Ohio University Press, 2008), 110.

8. A. Scott Berg, *Wilson* (New York: G. P. Putnam's Sons, 2013), 483.

9. "President Wilson Against Mob Spirit," *World Court* 4, no. 1 (1918), 506.

10. James Weldon Johnson, *Writings*, 493.

Chapter 29: Warren G. Harding

1. Matthew Rees, *From the Deck to the Sea: Blacks and the Republican Party* (Wakefield, NH: Longwood Academic, 1991), 122.

2. W. E. B. Du Bois, *The Crisis* 23, no. 2 (December 1921): 56.

3. W. E. B. Du Bois, *The Crisis* 24, no. 1 (May 1922): 11, accessed May 13, 2017.

4. John W. Dean, *Warren G. Harding: The 29th President, 1921–1923* (American Presidents Series) (New York: Times Books, 2004), 124–25.

Chapter 30: Calvin Coolidge

1. David Greenberg, *Calvin Coolidge: The 30th President, 1923–1929* (American Presidents Series) (New York: Times Books, 2006), 87.
2. Kenneth O'Reilly, *Nixon's Piano: Presidents and Racial Politics from Washington to Clinton* (New York: Free Press, 1995), 100.
3. Samuel O'Dell, "Blacks, the Democratic Party, and the Presidential Election of 1928: A Mild Rejoinder," *Phylon* 48, no. 1 (1987): 10, https://doi.org/10.2307/274997.

Chapter 31: Herbert Hoover

1. David Burner, *Herbert Hoover: A Public Life* (New York: Knopf, 1979), 27.
2. Herbert Hoover, *Principles of Mining: Valuation, Organization and Administration; Copper, Gold, Lead, Silver, Tin and Zinc* (New York and London: McGraw-Hill, 1909), 163.
3. O'Reilly, *Nixon's Piano*, 105.
4. O'Reilly, *Nixon's Piano*, 108.

Chapter 32: Franklin D. Roosevelt

1. Carl Thomas Rowan, *Dream Makers, Dream Breakers: The World of Justice Thurgood Marshall* (New York: Welcome Rain, 2002), 132.
2. Eleanor Roosevelt, "Freedom: Promise or Fact," *Negro Digest* 1 (October 1, 1943), https://socialwelfare.library.vcu.edu/issues/discrimination/freedom-promise-of-fact-1943.

Chapter 33: Harry S. Truman

1. David McCullough, *Truman* (New York: Simon & Schuster, 2003), 45.
2. William E. Leuchtenburg, *In the Shadow of FDR: From Harry Truman to Barack Obama* (Ithaca, NY, and London: Cornell University Press, 2009), 26.
3. Paul Robeson, *Paul Robeson Speaks: Writings, Speeches, and Interviews, a Centennial Celebration* (New York: Citadel Press, 1978), 173–76.
4. Gary A. Donaldson, "Who Wrote the Clifford Memo? The Origins of Campaign Strategy in the Truman Administration," *Presidential Studies Quarterly* 23, no. 4 (1993): 747–54.
5. Samuel Walker, *Presidents and Civil Liberties from Wilson to Obama: A Story of Poor Custodians* (New York: Cambridge University Press, 2012), 146–47.
6. Michael Gardner, *Harry Truman and Civil Rights: Moral Courage and Political Risks* (Carbondale and Edwardsville: Southern Illinois University Press, 2002), 138–39.
7. "Harry S. Truman: Address in Harlem, New York, Upon Receiving the Franklin Roosevelt Award," accessed January 2, 2017, https://www.presidency.ucsb.edu/docments/address-harlem-new-york-upon-receiving-the-franklin-roosevelt-award.
8. *Courier-Journal* (Louisville, KY), March 20, 1960: 1, accessed May 13, 2017, http://www.newspapers.com/image/107981129/?terms=louisville%2Bcourier%2Bjournal%2Bharry%2Btruman.
9. Raymond H. Geselbracht, ed., *Civil Rights Legacy of Harry S. Truman* (Kirksville, MO: Truman State University Press, 2007), 90, https://socialwelfare.library.vcu.edu/issues/discrimination/freedom-promise-of-fact-1943.
10. Dean Acheson, "Unpublished Letters from Dean Acheson to Ex-President Harry Truman," *American Heritage*, June 27, 1960, http://www.americanheritage.com/content/dear-boss?page=4.

Chapter 34: Dwight D. Eisenhower

1. David A. Nichols, *A Matter of Justice: Eisenhower and the Beginning of the Civil Rights Revolution* (New York: Simon & Schuster, 2007), 52.

2. Nichols, *A Matter of Justice*, 70.
3. Milton S. Katz, "E. Frederick Morrow and Civil Rights in the Eisenhower Administration," *Phylon* 42, no. 2 (1981): 133, https://doi.org/10.2307/274718.
4. E. Frederic Morrow, *Black Man in the White House* (Cork: BookBaby, 2014), 275.
5. Clayborne Carson, Susan Carson, Adrienne Clay, Virginia Shadron, and Kieran Taylor (eds.), *The Papers of Martin Luther King, Jr: Symbol of the Movement, January 1957– December 1958* (Berkeley and Los Angeles: University of California Press, 2000), 278.
6. O'Reilly, *Nixon's Piano*, 179.
7. O'Reilly, *Nixon's Piano*, 170.
8. Earl Warren, *The Memoirs of Earl Warren* (New York: Doubleday, 1977), 291.

Chapter 35: John F. Kennedy
1. John Kirk, *Martin Luther King Jr.* (Profiles in Power Series) (Abingdon, UK, and New York: Routledge, 2013), 54.
2. Nick Bryant, *The Bystander: John F. Kennedy and the Struggle for Black Equality* (New York: Basic Books, 2006), 225–26.
3. Bryant, *The Bystander*, 231.
4. David J. Garrow, *Bearing the Cross: Martin Luther King, Jr., and the Southern Christian Leadership Conference* (New York: Vintage Books, 1988), 162.
5. Bryant, *The Bystander*, 423.
6. Garrow, *Bearing the Cross*, 271.
7. Richard Reeves, *President Kennedy: Profile of Power* (New York: Simon & Schuster, 1994), 571.
8. Garrow, *Bearing the Cross*, 285.

Chapter 36: Lyndon B. Johnson
1. Robert Parker and Richard L. Rashke, *Capitol Hill in Black and White* (New York: Jove, 1989), 52.
2. Garrow, *Bearing the Cross*, 347–50.
3. O'Reilly, *Nixon's Piano*, 248–50.

Chapter 37: Richard M. Nixon
1. O'Reilly, *Nixon's Piano*, 287.
2. Booker, *The Black Presidential Nightmare*, 578.
3. Clarence Lusane, *The Black History of the White House* (San Francisco: City Lights Books, 2013), 311.

Chapter 38: Gerald R. Ford
1. Booker, *The Black Presidential Nightmare*, 560.
2. *Public Papers of the Presidents of the United States: Gerald R. Ford, 1976–1977* (Washington, DC: Government Printing Office, 1980), 1799.

Chapter 39: Jimmy Carter
1. Jimmy Carter, interview with the *New York Daily News*, April 12, 1976.
2. Kenneth E. Morris, *Jimmy Carter, American Moralist* (Athens: University of Georgia Press, 1997), 85.
3. Alexander P. Lamis, ed., *Southern Politics in the 1990s* (Baton Rouge: LSU Press, 1999), 8.
4. Paul Frymer, *Uneasy Alliances: Race and Party Competition in America* (Princeton Studies in American Politics) (Princeton, NJ: Princeton University Press, 1999), 166–67.

Chapter 40: Ronald Reagan
1. *Desert Sun* (Palm Springs, CA), May 12, 1966, California Digital Newspaper Collection, accessed February 25, 2017, https://cdnc.ucr.edu/cgi-bin/cdnc?a=d&d=DS19660512.2.2.

2. O'Reilly, *Nixon's Piano*, 366.
3. O'Reilly, *Nixon's Piano*, 368.

Chapter 41: George H. W. Bush

1. Frymer, *Uneasy Alliances*, 101.
2. Dan Fesperman, "Sun Reporter Aided Thomas, Book Says," *Baltimore Sun*, June 2, 1992.

Chapter 42: Bill Clinton

1. Toni Morrison, "On the First Black President," *New Yorker*, October 5, 1998, http://www.newyorker.com/magazine/1998/10/05/comment-6543.
2. Frymer, *Uneasy Alliances*, 5.
3. Bill Clinton and Albert Gore, *Putting People First: How We Can All Change America* (New York: Times Books, 1992), 64.
4. "Bill Clinton's Stone Mountain Moment," accessed June 15, 2019, https://jacobinmag.com/2016/09/stone-mountain-kkk-white-supremacy-simmons.
5. Thomas B. Edsall, "Black Leaders View Clinton Strategy with Mix of Pragmatism, Optimism," *Washington Post*, October 28, 1992, https://www.washingtonpost.com/archive/politics/1992/10/28/black-leaders-view-clinton-strategy-with-mix-of-pragmatism-optimism/4fb1805b-5ecd-4106-ae5a-f4e9fed46eb6/?utm_term=.da63d880f79b.
6. "The Lani Guinier Mess," *New York Times*, June 5, 1993, http://www.nytimes.com/1993/06/05/opinion/the-lani-guinier-mess.html.
7. Michele Simon, "Food Stamps: Follow the Money," 2012, http://www.eatdrinkpolitics.com/wp-content/uploads/FoodStampsFollowtheMoneySimon.pdf.
8. Connie A. Miller, *Frederick Douglass: American Hero and International Icon of the Nineteenth Century* (Bloomington, IN: Xlibris, 2008), 277.

Chapter 43: George W. Bush

1. Thomas W. Benson and Brian J. Snee (eds.), *The Rhetoric of the New Political Documentary* (Carbondale: Southern Illinois University Press, 2008), 132.
2. Elisabeth Bumiller, *Condoleezza Rice: An American Life* (New York: Random House, 2009), 45.

Chapter 44: Barack Obama

1. "In Their Own Words: Obama on Reagan," *New York Times*, January 21, 2008, http://www.nytimes.com/ref/us/politics/21seelye-text.html.
2. "Obama's Father's Day Remarks," *New York Times*, June 15, 2008, https://www.nytimes.com/2008/06/15/us/politics/15text-obama.html.
3. "Transcript: Barack Obama's Speech on Race," NPR.org, March 18, 2008, http://www.npr.org/templates/story/story.php?storyId=88478467.
4. Fredrick C. Harris, *The Price of the Ticket: Barack Obama and the Rise and Decline of Black Politics* (Oxford, UK, and New York: Oxford University Press, 2014), 173.

Chapter 45: Donald Trump

1. Bob Woodward, *Fear: Trump in the White House* (London: Simon & Schuster, 2018), 275.
2. "Warren Criticizes 'Class' Parades," *New York Times*, June 1, 1927, https://timesmachine.nytimes.com/timesmachine/1927/06/01/96649934.pdf.
3. Woodward, *Fear*, 246.

ACKNOWLEDGMENTS

I thank my *Black Agenda Report* co-founders, Glen Ford and the late Bruce Dixon, whose mentorship and encouragement made such an impact on my life and on my growth as a writer. Along with the *Black Agenda Report* team of Nellie Bailey, Ajamu Baraka, Ann Garrison, Danny Haiphong, Anthony Monteiro and Roberto Sirvent, they have been steadfast supporters over the years.

Mark Crispin Miller and Jon Jeter provided excellent advice and counsel to a novice book author. The National Writers Union, especially Susan E. Davis, were instrumental in assisting me as I navigated a process that was new to me.

Randall Wallace, the Tides Foundation, and the Institute for Media Analysis provided much needed support which made this project possible.

I relied upon the New York Public Library and the Library of Congress as I undertook the task of researching every American presidential administration. Both institutions are invaluable to authors and to the public at large.

Chip Fleischer and Devin Wilkie of Steerforth Press showed confidence in my work and guided me in the process of improving this book. I am very grateful for all their help.